Mellow Peaches, Three Pounds for a Dollar

Matthew D. Olerio

PublishAmerica
Baltimore

© 2003 by Matthew D. Olerio.
All rights reserved. No part of this book may be reproduced, stored in a retrieval system or transmitted in any form or by any means without the prior written permission of the publishers, except by a reviewer who may quote brief passages in a review to be printed in a newspaper, magazine or journal.

First printing

For bulk orders of Mellow Peaches, please call 1-800-741-7707 or e-mail your request to www.mellowpeaches.com.

ISBN: 1-4137-2748-4
PUBLISHED BY PUBLISHAMERICA, LLLP
www.publishamerica.com
Baltimore

Printed in the United States of America

For my Marjorie, Matthew Jr., James and Shayna

……..Mom and Dad too!

Cover design; David LaChance Jr., Providence, R.I.
Front cover [green truck painting]: Artist, Joseph Reboli, Long Island, NY
Back cover photo [me], Kathleen Lombardi, North Kingstown, R.I.

Acknowledgements

Among my siblings, I am certainly not unique in achieving success, in every form of the word. There are six brothers and one sister in my family and each have made their own way and have realized their own impossible dreams and accomplishments. We have all learned from our parents that it is a sacred privilege and honor to be called a family. And with it comes an awesome responsibility and commitment to keep it together; so that generations to come will always know the intrinsic values of faith, love and family. I am most proud to be called an Olerio.

Thank you, Robin Fogg, for being the greatest neighbor in the world, for your relentless work and effort that went into this book and for reminding me what perseverance is all about. We love you and your beautiful family.

Thanks Dad for teaching me that hard work can overcome a multitude of mistakes.

Thank you Len Meyers for your prayers and incredible final edit.

Thank you Margie for always staying by my side, for your unwavering love, for being an incredible wife and mom, and for being so courageous.

Thank you, Lord!

Preface

I remember my father saying to me when I was a teenager, "There are three types of people in this world; those who make things happen, those who watch things happen, and those who wonder what the heck happened...which one are you?" I always thought that it was my dad's original line until I found out differently many years later, but never-the-less, at that particular moment, I looked down at the ground, stared at my shoes, pondered the question for a few seconds, then looked up at him and said, "Well, I certainly don't plan on being the last two types, that's for sure!"

Throughout my life, I have looked upon that candid assessment made by my dad of those three types of people and have done everything in my power to be the guy who "makes things happen!" Quite honestly, I'm glad I took that road, although it hasn't always been the smoothest one to travel. I'm what you might call, "a dreamer," but I'm a dreamer who has learned what it takes to make the dream come true and see it through to completion, even when the shadows of doubt crept in and tried to throw me off course.

A few years ago a good friend asked me point blank, "Matt, what is it about you that it comes so natural to step out, take these seemingly huge risks, to pursue your dreams and not be afraid to fail and fall flat on your face?"

I sat back, pondered the question for a moment and then said, "I love being challenged. I find it exciting and exhilarating. If I don't feel like I am creating, then I don't feel that I am fulfilled. I think I've learned to harness the basic elements: desire, courage, determination, perseverance, and commitment to take risks. As far as me not being afraid to fail and fall...I've been a lot more afraid than you might think, but my desire to accomplish my goals and realize my dreams has always been far greater than my fear of failure." I then said with a big smile, "I can teach you how to step out and take on your greatest dreams and goals."

While many dreamers have similar desires, some individuals pursue their dreams with reckless abandon using all the strength and desire they can muster and dive head first into accomplishing their goals, while others sit back and look for the perfect timing, the perfect setting, the approval of friends and family, but never end up getting their dream off the ground or even off the paper on which they've so meticulously detailed them.

Perhaps you're ready to finally take hold of your dream, put your full potential into action and say, "Don't tell me it can't be done, I'm going for it!" Or perhaps you're ready to say, "I'm going to be the one who makes things happen!" Maybe you have an idea to start your own business, create an invention, enter the Olympics, go back to college, run for public office, go into the mission fields of a third-world country, or follow through once and for all, on a childhood dream. Whatever your goals may be, it's what's in your heart that matters most. Whatever your dreams and goals are, if you want to realize them, and qualify as a legitimate dream contender, then it's time to act on your dreams. Real dreamers have similar ambitions and desires that speak to their hearts with an undefined passion saying, "I'm willing to take the risk and put in the time to get there. I won't settle for mediocrity, I want to be all I was put on this earth to be. I want to see my potential realized in my life's work."

When I decided to write *Mellow Peaches, Three Pounds for a Dollar*, my goal was to write about my entrepreneurial experiences and present realistic, down-to-earth formulas and strategies for accomplishing incredible goals that seem impossible to achieve and more importantly, to challenge the reader to realize the full-blown version of the American Dream and discover that the possibilities for your life are endless. I have learned through my experiences that God has blessed each one of us with exciting and unique gifts and talents. How, or if we choose to use our talents, is yet another story. While applying your talents through faith and perseverance you can awaken the spirit inside you that can move mountains and calm the roughest seas. When your dreams are achieved through the use of your talents, you will find fulfillment.

I firmly believe that hard work, courage, and perseverance can overcome adversity and humble beginnings. I also believe that a dream can unfold as you begin to put certain basic principles into motion in your life. The question is: "Are you ready to stop thinking that you have to measure up to others who you look upon as successful and to start focusing on your own potential strengths? Are you ready to stop talking about soaring like and eagle, and finally buckle yourself in for the ride of your life?"

An individual will sometimes search for years for what he or she thinks they need to make them happy and successful and will usually return home to find it. In *Mellow Peaches, Three Pounds for a Dollar* I'm asking you to come home and find your dream. Find out who you really are and who you were truly meant to be. Once you do, amazing things will happen, and "windows of opportunity" will no longer be just a nice yuppie cliché. It will be a way of life.

The key ingredients to becoming successful with any personal achievement require a solid game plan and strategy, intestinal fortitude and tenacity, along with a faith in God, especially when your family, friends, and colleagues start telling you that you have gone off the deep end and you're not thinking clearly because you're about to give your boss a two-week notice from your cushy job and chase some crazy dream.

So, for all those dream seekers looking for more than a 9-5 job, who are willing to tap into their unlimited potential and who are looking for a more than the "Yes sir, no ma'am" corporate play-the-game-to-survive routine, I offer you *Mellow Peaches, Three Pounds for a Dollar*. On the day that you decide to step out and leave your comfort zone and pursue your lifelong dream, and everyone looks at you in bewilderment and asks, "WHY?" you can look them in the eye with a confident, sly, but sure smile and say, "Mellow Peaches, Three Pounds for a Dollar."

After you read my story, I hope and expect that you will gain the confidence to accomplish more than you ever dreamed possible and unlock all the amazing dreams stored up inside you. Dream your greatest dream and watch it all come true right before your eyes.

Go for it, friend! Live your dream! You'll never regret one day of it.

God bless you,
Matthew Olerio

Chapter One

The Entrepreneur in All of Us

"When I was a boy of 14, my father was so ignorant; I could hardly stand to have the old man around. But when I got to be 21, I was astonished at how much the old man had learned in seven years."
Mark Twain

I grew up in the '60s, a second-generation Italo-American, in the little Italy section of Providence, Rhode Island. I was the fifth child in a family of seven children, six boys and one girl. My dad, a cross between Al Capone and Marlon Brando, ruled as strong as any Italian dictator-dad in the land. Extra large, intimidating brown eyes were his trademark. One cold stare from dad was enough to stop anyone dead in their tracks; any of my friends' "tough dads" paled in comparison. Any new friend who visited our home soon figured out that a "Hello, Mr. Olerio," was offered strictly out of respect and knew that no response would come their way.

Feeding a family of nine daily, including six boys who all grew to be over six feet tall, was no easy task for both parents, but they managed and we never went without. Many of what my mom would refer to today as "peasant dishes" would feed the entire family for just a few dollars. My mom taught me how to stretch out limited resources, by using my imagination. We didn't have a lot of money, but we had family and lots of it. A birthday party, first communion, confirmation, the annual feast of the Blessed Mother, would create a joyous entourage of grandparents, cousins, aunts and uncles that could be heard from blocks away. My sister referred to us as, "The-loud-family-that-ate-well." No matter what the topic of discussion, whether it was politics, sports, careers, or family matters, the conversation always reverted back to food. It came as no surprise that the food industry was where I would start my first business as a young man; it just came naturally.

When it came to work, our dad had an infamous line that he used on a regular basis. He'd say, "You want anything in this life, then you gotta GRIND, you gotta SWEAT, you gotta work twelve-hour days." As a young boy, I knew what "sweat" meant, but "grind" stumped me for quite some time.

Your first entrepreneurial experience probably took place during your teenage years. At age thirteen, my entrepreneurial juices started flowing. My first taste of being self-employed, consisted of a paper route with over one hundred customers. I was a faithful, diligent, paperboy in rain, sleet, and snow. My customers entrusted me with their secret hiding spots to put their newspaper and collect my weekly fees and tips. Soon they hired me to cut their grass, rake their leaves, and shovel snow from their driveways. As the long Rhode Island winters came to an end, I'd offer the finest, cheapest spring clean-up in town. I was even a baby-sitter for the same customers.

One night my older brother who worked at Maria's, an Italian restaurant/banquet hall about a mile from our home, came down with a fever. My mom called Maria to tell her that he was ill. Since he was Maria's hardest worker, like my two older brothers before him, she was devastated and desperate for someone to fill the vacant position for the night. My Italian mom said to a very distraught, Italian Maria, "My fourteen year old son, Matthew, is available tonight; he's a good worker, Maria."

Maria paused, thought about my age and the fact that I didn't have working papers and said, "Have him at the restaurant by four o'clock."

My first night on the job turned out to be washing dishes for a wedding of one hundred-sixty people. It was sometime during that first evening at Maria's Restaurant at age fourteen, somewhere in between the Italian wedding soup and countless dishes of mashed potatoes and half-eaten roasted chickens thrown at me, that I decided that working, "like a dog," washing dishes, solo for $1.40 per hour, as I listened to some Frank Sinatra/Paul Anka wannabe, sing a limited repertoire of "My Way," "Tiny Bubbles," and "Put Your Head on my Shoulders," was clearly not the career direction I wanted to pursue. I did the math and quickly realized I could make more money cutting just three lawns in my neighborhood, than I could make working all week at Maria's; not to mention I didn't have to come home smelling like a wet dog with dishpan hands at one o'clock in the morning. I was determined to stick to my self-employed mentality. I had experienced my first real taste of what I thought, "You gotta sweat, you gotta grind," meant, and I was determined to "grind" my way to a better job and earn more money.

At age fifteen I became a door-to-door salesman. Our neighbor was one of those fanatic salesman/distributors of an Amway-like product line. He quickly spotted my natural ambition to make a buck and recruited me into his pyramid sales fold, working on straight commission for each case of cleaning supplies I sold.

When I first walked down the stairs into his basement and saw the hundreds of cases of "ZIF" cleaner, I said to myself, "YEAH, Ok, Matt, now you're going to rake in the big bucks!"

Some feel it takes courage to go door to door, but I was too caught up in the thought of making a buck and actually enjoyed the challenge. As I look back, selling door to door brought out some definitive personal traits. Like any other sales job, cold calling door to door was often met with rejection. I quickly learned that an immediate "NO!" didn't always mean a definite "NO." My boyish charm and persuasive personality often helped me overcome the initial rejection and close the sale. My persistence, determination and a big smile after my sales pitch were more often than not rewarded with, "OK, young man, I'll try one bottle."

My immediate response was, "Well, ok, but you know you can save $3.00 if you buy two bottles!"

However, my Zif career was short-lived. I was literally touting this product door to door to everyone in my neighborhood. The Fuller Brush salesman had nothing over me as I enthusiastically and methodically knocked on every door within a ten-block radius. I was so confident in what my neighbor told me this product could do, that I was ready to sell every paper route customer at least two bottles. I stopped selling this universal wonder cleaner after experiencing my first rude awakening. That fateful day came when I decided to challenge a neighbor, Mr. Nash, to a duel on his white wall tires. He was out in his driveway washing his car and was using the newly acclaimed, all purpose cleaner, Fantastic. I quickly gave him my sales pitch. "Mr. Nash," I said with complete confidence, "ZIF will make your teeth white as well as your whitewall tires. It will clean and shine your kitchen floor, bathroom tile, revitalize your brass and silver and relieve heartburn."

Mr. Nash looked me right in the eyes as if to say, "Kid, what are you, nuts or something?" Then he quickly dropped to one knee and effortlessly sprayed his cleaner on one whitewall tire and Zif on another. I lost decisively as the Fantastic cleaned his white walls with relative ease while my magical ZIF failed and I floundered.

I went home with my tail between my legs never to sell ZIF again, or any other product for that matter that I did not believe in. I figured anything that claimed to clean your teeth and your tile, had to have some drawbacks. Mr. Nash's whitewall tires convinced me that if a product couldn't deliver the results, it would soon fade away from the market.

I decided to make another attempt at working for local businesses and went through the normal, multiple career changes of the teenage years. These included my mastering the line, "waiting on a hot fry," at the local burger joint, washing sheet pans and mixing dough at the corner bakery, stacking shelves at the local supermarket and bussing tables at the local ice cream parlor, while the waitresses scooped up the big bucks (No pun intended).

By age sixteen my father's infamous line came popping into in my brain, "You gotta sweat, you gotta grind. If you want anything in this life you have to work for it, you have to put in twelve-hour days." By this time, my older brother, Al and I had it with clock-punching jobs. We were both sadly mistaken to think that those types of jobs were better than our earlier self-employed career days of mowing lawns, shoveling snow, and raking leaves. We were also getting older, looking ahead to college and needing to make the "big money." We were now willing to heed our father's advice. However, we were also determined to find a better and smarter way to "grind" our way to financial success.

Chapter Two

Tony, Dad & Horseshoe Crabs

"When There Is No Wind ...Row."
            Latin Proverb

In May of 1973, just three weeks before our high school summer vacation, my dad looked my brother and me in the eyes, and said quite emphatically, "When your mother and I return from my business conference in Florida in late June, you better have found a summer job."

"Oh, yes, Dad," I remember saying to myself so brazenly, "We'll have a job all right, because we have a plan."

The first moment of our summer vacation, as soon as school was out, my brother and I decided it was time to implement our plan. We had our eyes on an old homemade 19 foot boat built by a retired navy man. He was getting on in years and decided it was time to sell it and part with the old girl. Oddly enough, it was in the shape of a PT boat. We didn't care one iota, about its unorthodox appearance. We were going to convert it into a quahog skiff, and use it for bull raking quahogs {New England clams; Kawhawgs} and rake in the big bucks. So, with every penny we could scrape together, with every dollar we had ever saved and with all the money we could borrow, we bought the homemade PT boat. Then we purchased a used forty-five-horsepower Johnson outboard engine. Next, we ordered the finest twenty-five-foot bull rake that money could buy from the living legends within the quahog community, the Maddelina brothers. We had one big problem. The PT boat leaked like a sieve and needed some heavy-duty repair work. We knew as much about boat repair and fiber glassing techniques as we did about bull raking, [nothing], but we were so determined and excited about our new venture that we set out to repair the ole' girl with unabashed enthusiasm and a clear focus on what we wanted to accomplish that summer.

Before our parents left for Florida, Dad had a new asphalt driveway installed. My brother and I, not knowing the molecular tendencies of freshly installed asphalt, combined with ninety-degree days, had innocently placed our new warship on cinder blocks in the driveway directly in front of our garage in order to give our boat all the needed TLC and repairs before its first launching. It was my dad who undoubtedly fostered the entrepreneurial spirit within me and my brother, so naturally, we figured that he would be proud of us, once he came back from Florida.

Thirty years later, I can still see my dad's facial expression as he and my mom pulled into the driveway; eyes bulging out of his head and my mom's fear for us in her eyes. There was our boat, our pride and joy, sitting on a very comfortable forty-five- degree slant with the cinder blocks deeply embedded (more like melted) into the fresh asphalt.

"What the hell is this?" my dad yelled out with just one foot barely out of the car door.

I wasted no time. I stood up, inside the boat, safely away from arms length and stared down at my dad. Covered with fiberglass, paint and dirt, I spoke in my most manly voice possible, "We're going to quahog, Dad, and we're working for ourselves this summer."

"Yeah," my brother quickly chimed in, "There's big money in quahogging, big money."

After the shock of the boat and the sunken driveway had set in and generated a few choice words from our dad, he said in an exasperated whisper, "There's no money in quahogs, you should peddle fruits and vegetables instead."

Three days later our boat was launched into the beautiful Atlantic Ocean's Narragansett Bay. We were about to embark on our first real entrepreneurial experience outside of our neighborhood and comfort zone. Our first week at sea was frustrating to say the least, but my brother and I were determined. We were on the boat by sunrise each morning in search of the best quahog spots in the bay. We followed the pros, the veterans, who shell fished for a living, 365 days a year. Wherever they went, we tagged along and found a spot just close enough to learn from them and far enough away to not get on their nerves or tick them off.

Letting a twenty-five- foot bull rake into the water and then pulling up eighty pounds of mud was no easy task; believe me it's not called a bull rake for nothing. While the veterans were pulling in full baskets of little necks (the smallest of the quahog family and most lucrative to catch), my brother and I continued to pull up the extra large variety of quahog, the kind that brought in very little money. We also continued to bring up tons of mud, as well as a countless number of horseshoe crabs, which were worthless. Horseshoe crabs are the oldest known sea creatures, dating back to prehistoric times. To us they were a constant reminder that we were failing miserably in our new venture.

When we went home at night the first words out of dear old dad's mouth were, "How much money did you bring in today?"

Our answers for the first few weeks were usually similar, "Uh, we made $32 today, but the water was too calm. We couldn't get the right rhythm going to make a big catch."

At this point, it would have been easier for us to quit or for Dad to draw the line, however, we were taught to persevere. After a week of our excuses, our dad, never worried about embarrassing us, or bothered by what others might think of his parenting skills, saw that we were struggling, and in his own stubborn way, he wanted to help us.

Dad told my older brother Al to get in the car. He proceeded to drive him up to the Oakland Beach fishing docks where many of the local shell fishermen docked their boats and hung out. It just so happened that several fisherman were sitting on the docks chugging down some beers after a hard day's work. My dad, with Al trailing behind, walked up to them. Dad wasted no time, and with a cigarette hanging from his mouth asked, "You guys quahog, right?"

They all kind of half nodded their heads yes as if to say, "No, we're taking sewing classes."

However, they showed no signs of disrespect. I'm sure they figured any guy that comes down to the docks dressed in a suit and who looks like Al Capone might be a little whacked out and not the type you mess with or laugh at.

My dad then said, "My sons are bull raking for the summer to earn money for college. Can you teach them the ropes?"

By this time my brother, all 6'4" and 235 pounds of him, felt like a ten-year-old kid having his dad take him to school and wanted to literally crawl under the docks. The last thing he wanted was to be brought in front of a tough crowd of shell fishermen with his daddy as his spokesperson, and the last thing the shell fishermen wanted was any more competition out in the bay especially from some young, green, college kids.

"Uh, sure," they said with a sort of devious smile, "send them down one morning and we'll teach them everything."

Needless to say, my brother and I never showed up for our fishing lesson.

By the third week my dad's patience grew thin. One evening in his ever-calming, loud voice, he began, "You better start finding another way to make more money, because your quahogging venture is quickly becoming a bust proposition. You should do your quahogging in the morning and get a second job in the afternoon." At that point we had no choice but to evaluate our past successes. Out came the lawn mowers from our garage and we soon became shell fishermen by morning and landscapers by afternoon and evening.

One morning, just after sunrise, the fog and haze were lifting from the water, and the bay looked like one massive steam bath. Suddenly, from out of nowhere, like an angel from heaven, a veteran quahogger drifted over to our boat. He signaled to me to catch his rope as he pulled his professional, shiny, red and white quahog skiff up alongside our homemade PT boat that was painted battleship gray and still leaked like a sieve. His name was Tony, a deaf mute, with biceps and forearms that were the size of tree trunks. Tony was a living legend among quahoggers, the king, the Mohammed Ali of littleneck bull rakers, the Elvis of the Narragansett Bay shell fishermen, and here he was on our homemade, leaky PT boat.

The first thing he did was signal to us to slide our bull rake into the water on the starboard side of the boat. Then he took control of the bull rake handles. He motioned for us to step aside and pay attention. With a circular, thrusting rhythm that was like watching poetry in motion, he began to teach two rookies the ropes and bull raking 101. We could literally hear the faint sound of the littlenecks clashing into the metal rake as the beautiful sound traveled up the long metal pole from twenty or so feet below the ocean. Within a few minutes he started the upward pull of the long expansion pole that housed the rake on the end. All I could notice were Tony's massive arms with muscles on top of muscles, bulging out as he pulled up the rake. When the rake finally came to the surface, he pulled it into the boat. There were more little necks in that one load than we had managed to catch in three hours on any given day.

He smiled as if to say, "Now that's how it's done." My brother and I laughed and high-fived each other like a couple of twelve-year-olds who had just won the Little League championship.

Tony had been watching us from his boat over the prior three weeks and realized that we were ambitious, hard-working young men with a lot of determination and guts, but without a clue about the shell fishing trade. He stayed on the boat for a good two hours teaching us and communicating with his hands and facial expressions. He showed us where the hot spots in the bay were, and how to work the hard ground where the little necks were more plentiful and explained with his hands to stay clear of the muddy bottoms. He also taught us to use the rougher water to our advantage and let the swaying of the boat work the bull rake. We were intrigued, inspired and blessed to have him on our boat teaching us the art of bull raking. Now, instead of making $32 per day we started to earn $60-$75 per day and some days close to $90.

I have often used his generosity as an illustration of how adults can serve as positive influences to youth or young men. Isn't it funny how certain people and specific moments stand the test of time and serve to alter the course of our life?

Someone once said that there are five influential people in our lives and seven major decisions that directly shape our future and impact our lives. My dad taught me at an early age to never give up, to persevere and work through adversity. Tony taught us that even the most strenuous bull work requires finesse and timing, along with the wisdom and sixth sense to try to always be in the right place at the right time. The horseshoe crabs taught us to laugh at ourselves when things weren't going according to plan and to press on, for a better catch.

Chapter Three

To Be or Not To Be ... an Entrepreneur?

"Don't ever come home with a full truck again!!!"
                                        Joseph Olerio

The summer of 1973 was almost half over. Although my brother and I had greatly improved our weekly revenues since learning the quahog trade, we knew that our dad was right. We needed to earn more money toward our college tuition. On several occasions, our father mentioned, that the best way to earn money, would be to peddle fruits and vegetables through the congested ethnic neighborhoods of Rhode Island. Without resisting his idea any longer, we put our boat up for sale and set out with our father to purchase a truck that we could use to sell the produce.

Everything quickly fell into place. Our first trip to check out a truck, being sold by a nearby tree farmer, turned into an instant purchase. She was a real beauty, a 1962 Ford three-quarter-ton stake body truck, green on green. She had four tires that I'm sure were left over retreads from World War II. Nevertheless, she ran like a charm and could carry some serious weight. My dad negotiated the price down from $1100 to $800. He explained so proudly that his two hard-working sons would be using it for peddling fruits and vegetables. I was certain the tree farmer was probably thinking, "This is 1973; nobody peddles fruits and vegetables through the streets anymore."

We gave him the cash, he smiled, gave us a firm handshake and off we went. The next day, a young man from our neighborhood heard about our shell fishing package: boat, engine, bull rake and bilge pump. He bought the dream package for $750.00. We broke even on our initial investment and the young man was excited to start a new career of his own.

In just a few short days we changed careers from quahoggers to fruit peddlers and we were ready for action. With no time to waste, we started off on our new endeavor. Our dad woke us up promptly at 4:30 A.M. He had a new sense of excitement about him. We got dressed and followed him, half asleep, in our '62 Ford truck to the downtown Providence Wholesale Produce Market, otherwise known as "The Market" or "The Walk." The Market was built right around the time of the Great Depression in 1929 and was the center of commerce for all wholesale produce in Southern New England. It was the length of one and one half football fields, made up of "stalls" or individual wholesale produce houses. These wholesale houses all competed against each other for business; but you always had a sense that the owners met privately in early-morning meetings to fix the prices.

As a teenager, my dad worked for several wholesale houses along, "The Walk" before joining the Navy in World War II and again, for a short time, after the war. He knew everyone there. He had worked side by side with several men unloading freight cars full of carrots, lettuce, and potatoes. You name it, he unloaded it. Many of the teenage kids he worked with in the late 1930s eventually worked their way up to become sales managers, shipping managers, or even owners at The Market. Dad began working for himself in the 1950s peddling and hustling produce on the corners of busy intersections. Our mom was always quick to point out that it rained every weekend for four straight weeks, when he first started. The money just wasn't coming in fast enough to support a large family. Reality set in and he had to quit before realizing the profits and success he knew were possible in the fruit and produce business.

Our first morning on "The Walk," as the sun started to rise, my brother and I were still waking up, Dad introduced us to his old buddies, while he was negotiating the purchases he was making on our behalf. My brother and I stood by the truck overwhelmed as pallets of produce were brought to us. Men were hustling and bustling up and down the ten-foot-wide loading docks with pallet jacks and forklifts. They were beeping their horns, arguing among themselves in one breath and laughing in another while loading up dozens of delivery trucks, symmetrically parked along the concrete loading docks of The Walk. Every ten minutes or so, one of the men would come up to us and say, "Are you the Olerios?" Half dazed, half overwhelmed, we would nod yes and they would drop another pallet of produce behind our truck.

Every few minutes our dad would come by half jogging, half walking, with a cigarette in one hand and purchase slips in the other. He started yelling out instructions to us on his way to yet another purchase. "C'mon, hurry up, load up the truck, and stack everything tight and neat."

Our dad was back. He was pumped. In his mind, he was twenty-five years old again and was ready to take on the entire state with his two entrepreneurial sons. It always seemed that my dad expected us to be the man he was meant to be. At that moment in time for my brother and me, our dad wanted us to be the fruit peddlers he never had the chance to become. I could see it in his eyes.

After loading and unloading the truck until it was to his exact liking, we eventually had a neat display of peaches, lettuce, green peppers, bananas, plums, sweet corn, potatoes, and cantaloupes. My dad obviously knew his produce; our display looked like an appealing farmer's market on wheels.

"All right," said Dad, "remember everything I told you, and head up to Federal Hill. Start near Spruce St., work your way up and down each street, toot the horn and yell out the window, "MELLOW PEACHES, THREE POUNDS FOR A DOLLAR!" He continued, "The peaches are your lead item, the peaches will get people to come out and buy other produce off the truck! Work hard and grind!"

My brother and I just nodded our heads with eagerness, excitement, and determination in our eyes. We looked over at the load on the truck with a sense of fear of the unknown and said, "Ok, Dad, thanks Dad, we'll see you tonight."

His last words that morning, as we pulled away from the loading docks were, "The load should take in approximately seven-hundred-fifty dollars, don't come back home until the truck is empty, don't forget..., yell loud."

About one-half mile away from the market, I hit a pothole in the road and three or four boxes of peaches went flying off the back of the truck. At thirty-eight pounds of peaches per box, the street looked like smashed peach cobbler. Cars and trucks could not help but drive over them. I stopped the truck and got out to assess the damage. I definitely wished that I had kept going. The morning rush hour traffic heading into downtown Providence slowed down to a crawl. Onlookers gawked at us while their tires mashed the four hundred or so peaches lying in the road. I'm sure they thought we were a couple of Italian immigrants who had just landed at the port of Providence a few days earlier.

My brother decided to ride in the back bed of the truck to stop anything else from falling off. He climbed up on the tailgate; spread his arms out in a full stretch side to side, while firmly gripping each end of the truck's green wooden stakes. I stayed in the right lane of Interstate 95 barely traveling thirty-five miles per hour with the gas pedal to the floor. Our 1962 stake body truck was loaded to the max with produce and swaying from side to side while tilted back on a severe angle with the tire rims touching the ground and an eighteen year old guy who was 6'4", 235 pounds, spread eagle trying to hold on to the load. Cars passed us and passengers stared at us as if we were from another planet. We didn't care. We were so caught up in getting off the road to safety we hardly noticed what a spectacular sight we were. Looking back on that first ride from the market, I realize now that my brother could have been instantly crushed to death, if that load had shifted and slid off the back of the truck in that traffic. Our mother always told us that we had God's favor and His angels were watching over us. I believed she was right that day. (I still do!)

Federal Hill, better know as The Hill, is a one-square-mile section of Providence. There my parents grew up, met each other, married, started a family. They lived in several tenement houses before they scraped enough money together to move on and raise their children elsewhere. It was and still is the "Little Italy" section of Rhode Island. The main strip was 100% Italian with roadside shops to buy everything from freshly killed chickens to slaughtered baby goats, which hung neatly in the shop windows. It was also known for some of the finest restaurants and bakeries in New England and had a reputation for other exciting "things" as well. The side streets were made up of two and three tenement homes closely stacked together in rows. By the early 1970s, the neighborhood was clearly starting to show signs of wear and tear. Many of the homes were still neatly kept, filled with a combination of large Italian families and old-timers who had lived there since the early 1900's. Italians love their fresh produce and since my brother and I looked like two young guys direct from Rome, it was a natural match.

With the produce in place we started to drive through the streets of The Hill. I started to toot the horn with anticipated excitement, then I turned to my brother and said, "Go ahead and yell mellow peaches, three pounds for a dollar, just like Dad said."

My brother looked at me as if I had two heads and quickly said, "I'm not yelling mellow peaches out the window; you yell."

I responded back to him with a half laugh, half smile, "I'm not yelling it, you yell it; I'm the driver, the horn man."

The morning passed. Sales were slower than slow. The little money we took in from the morning we used to buy a couple of great Italian grinders (a large Rhode Island submarine sandwich). The afternoon produced similar results, an occasional sale here and there. We soon started to think that bull raking for quahogs was a lot better and a lot more profitable. We were now convinced our dad was wrong. Peddling was a dying art from the past. People were not going to buy from a fruit peddler anymore.

We headed home around 6:00 P.M, tired and discouraged with approximately $90.00 of the $750.00 we were supposed to take in from the load. Like something out of Hollywood movie in slow motion, we pulled down our street and could see our dad waiting for us in the driveway by the side door still dressed in his suit. He was pacing back and forth, while smoking a cigarette. My brother and I looked at each other and without saying a word we knew exactly what was coming. I pulled in the driveway as my dad's bulging eyes were fixed on the back of the truck, which was now a very sloppy three fourths of the way full. "What the hell is this?" He yelled out loud enough to be heard a block away.

I stepped out of the truck, threw my arms up in the air and quickly said, "No one wanted to buy from us, Dad."

My brother promptly added, "I don't think this peddling is going to work, Dad. This is 1973, not 1933."

My dad's veins started to pop out of his neck and his extra large round head turned beet red. With fire in his eyes and what we thought looked like smoke coming out of his ears, he looked us both in the eyes and said with teeth clenched, "Get back in the truck; I'll be right out."

In the meantime, Mom poked her head out the kitchen window and said in her always supporting, calm voice, with a kind of, "I-feel-bad-for-you," expression on her face, "What happened, boys, business wasn't so good?"

"No, Mom," I said, "This peddling is a thing of the past."

All of a sudden grizzly bear Dad came banging out the side door dressed in some old set of clothes and a hat that looked like they had been in the cedar chest since he had peddled in the early fifties. "You," he quickly yelled out to my brother, "Climb back there and straighten out that mess." "You," he said to me in a horror movie, Jack Nicholson-type whispering voice, "Drive back up to The Hill."

It was one of the most memorable twenty-minute drives of my life as he started right in. "What did you guys do, sit on your butts and eat pizza all day?"

I wanted to tell him we had some great Italian grinders but didn't think it would go over too well. "Did you go where I told you?"

I nodded yes.

"Did you drive slowly down the streets? Did you toot the horn?"

Again, I nodded yes.

Then the big question came belting out of his mouth, "Did you yell out the window MELLOW PEACHES, THREE POUNDS FOR A DOLLAR?"

I drove with my eyes fixed straight ahead on the road and quietly said, "I was the driver and horn man, Al was supposed to yell out the window."

It was around 7:00 p.m. when we entered Federal Hill. My dad pointed me to a street where groups of people were hanging out on their porches relaxing from a hot summer day. He instructed me to stop and he quickly jumped out of the truck. He looked at my brother and me and started to yell out instructions, "You two bag and work the scales, I'll sell and collect the money."

At that very moment my dad became, "Joe the fruit peddler." He had a look in his eyes as if he was fighting for the heavyweight title. He was back in time; it was 1950 again as he started yelling toward the people in a baritone voice, hands cupped around his mouth, "MELLOW PEACHES, THREE POUNDS FOR A DOLLAR. MELLOW PEACHES, THREE POUNDS FOR A DOLLAR!"

For the next two hours, all my brother and I could do was follow our dad's lead, put our heads down and weigh and bag produce. As we watched in amazement, husbands, housewives, young and old alike, swarmed around our green stake body truck as if we were giving the stuff away. My brother and I continually climbed up and down the truck as we frantically ripped open new boxes of peaches, cantaloupes, peppers, bananas, replacing the empty boxes on the edge of the truck. People negotiated with my dad and he negotiated right back. "You want ten pounds of peaches?" he asked, "Give me three bucks." Or, "Give this nice young lady four pounds of peppers and let her taste a piece of that cantaloupe I just cut open; it's sweet as sugar."

By 9:00 p.m. our truck that was filled to capacity in the early morning hours, was completely empty. Not a single mellow peach could be found lying on the bed of the truck.

"Let's go home," Dad said with a smile as he gave me a light tap on the back of my head, as if to say, "That's how it's done!"

The ride home was filled with excitement as my brother and I were smiling from ear to ear. What a sense of accomplishment! What a feeling! What a night!!! We had taken in slightly under the $750.00 that my dad had said we would bring in. We were pumped, laughing, celebrating, high-fiving each other, feeling as if we were on top of the world. We were modern-day fruit peddlers.

Then about halfway home, Dad turned off the radio and began to speak with as much wisdom, firmness, kindness and advice as I had ever heard him use. He spoke to us like Don Corleone spoke to his son Michael, in their backyard garden, while sipping on red wine.

"Don't ever be afraid to be different! Don't ever be ashamed to yell out the window, especially when you have a great deal to offer. People will always swarm to a bargain and they'll always buy fresh produce, whether it's 1933 or 1973. I told you that you can make some serious money for yourselves peddling this summer. But, you have to work hard and work smart, and you have to grind." He ended with this line that is forever lodged in my mind, as he pointed his finger at us and his eyes became extra large again, "AND DON'T EVER COME HOME WITH A FULL TRUCK AGAIN."

For the remaining two months of the summer my brother and I became peddling machines. We were working harder than ever but this time, reaping the rewards. We were making $450.00 each per week. We became true-blue entrepreneurs.

I entitled this book, *Mellow Peaches, Three Pounds for a Dollar*, because that night, for me in the Federal Hill section of Providence, as a young man not yet seventeen years old, was a genuine turning point in my life. It was pivotal because that was the night I got the fever to be an entrepreneur. I was hooked. I carried that lesson with me well into my adult life and it inspired me into many successful endeavors, even into writing this book. This lesson taught me to never give up, and never be afraid to be different; if you believe wholeheartedly in something. That night taught me that hard work, determination, and good planning, incorporated with an appealing product at a good price, will always be rewarded.

For all who dream great dreams and pursue those dreams with reckless abandon, there lies the fear of yelling out of the truck window, the fear of being a little different, and going against the grain. The fear of the unknown, fear of failure, these fears taunt us and will usually get the best of us if we don't face them head on. Fear not…your truck can be emptied! You can yell out of that window. You don't have to settle for realizing only part of your goal or dream. Once you realize that your dream can come true, you too will have the desire, the courage, the determination and the chutzpah, to start yelling out of the window with your own unique style and passion.

Becoming the person you've always envisioned, requires certain action and mental exercises! Just as going on a diet to transform your body requires the action of eating the right foods and physical exercise. Goal setting is a proven technique for anyone that has a dream and a vision. Once you set these goals you must make an action plan to accomplish them with ferocity and vigor that you never thought you possessed.

My dad, Joseph Olerio
Mellowed, but still an intimidating figure at age 75!

Past Entrepreneurial Experiences

It's time to explore your own past entrepreneurial experiences. Recall your first paying jobs as a teenager; consider how you felt working for a boss/employer. Recall what lessons you learned about your self from these early positions. List the skills and personal characteristics that you possess that helped you succeed in previous jobs. These are the qualities that will help you succeed in future ventures.

_____
_____
_____
_____
_____
_____
_____
_____
_____
_____
_____
_____
_____
_____
_____
_____
_____
_____
_____
_____

Chapter Four

I Have a Plan

"A plan takes all your dreams and talents and maximizes them by bringing structure to the concept."
Bishop T.D. Jakes.

Perhaps you can recall someone, who has attempted some type of business for himself, or countless others with unrealized career possibilities or dreams, and they just fell short, overcome by the agony of defeat and failure. They had the talent, they had the dream, they were determined and committed, but for some reason or another, they failed. If it was an attempt at owning their own business or trying to develop an invention, maybe they stuck it out for a while, but the financial burdens and day-to-day pressures just became overwhelming and stressed them beyond what they could handle. As a result, they sold out, went bankrupt, gave up, or just plain closed the doors and went back to a, "real job."

These types of career failures are everyday occurrences in this world. They're as common as apple pie and Chevrolets. The big question is, why? Why do so many with good intentions, with great determination, courage, and a diligent commitment to their dream fall so short and never see their dream through to completion? The answer is in *The Great Investor* by T.D. Jakes. "They didn't have a solid plan." When there is no plan, even the greatest idea or the most talented of people will eventually succumb to failure because they didn't follow the blueprint, they went off course, and they didn't stay on the path. Memorize the following paragraph written by T.D. Jakes before you attempt anything.

The Power of a Plan:

"It's not enough to have a dream. A dream is a seed. The talent is important also as your dream cannot exceed your talent. But talent is water poured on a seed. As the seed must have water, the dream must be dreamed by someone with the talent to do what they are dreaming of or it cannot occur. But none of that is going to give long-term success without a plan. A plan takes all of your dreams and talents and maximizes them by bringing structure to the concept. A plan puts soil in the pot, plants the seed, and regulates the temperature and watering schedule so that the seed becomes a healthy plant."

I can tell you first hand, every time I have pursued an idea, chased a dream, dived in head first with tenacity, courage, and pure determination, but did not take the time to develop a solid game plan, I have fallen flat on my face. Plans should be adjusted as you gain wisdom and confidence and come up with better ideas to accomplish your dream, but you need the original blueprint before you can start knocking down walls and moving closet doors.

We are driven by our dreams! The dream is the spark that starts our engine each day and keeps our engine running throughout the day. It's what motivates us to get out of bed and say, Ok, yesterday was not such a good day, but today I'm moving forward, I'm not looking back and I'm not focusing on the negative. The dream motivates us, for sure, but it's the plan that moves the dream along.

Martin Luther King Jr. had a dream, but he also had one heck of a plan. Even in his infamous "I Have a Dream" speech, at the Washington Monument in 1963, he prophesied, "I might not get there with you." You see his plan was so detailed that he even knew his days were numbered, but his dream came true and the dream still lives on and on and on.

My dad had a dream for us to peddle fruits and vegetables, and he also had a plan. He knew the right areas to canvas and knew exactly what to buy and say to attract customers. Did we alternate his plan to fit our style? Of course we did. In some cases sticking to an original plan blindly just for the sake of sticking to the plan, can be as foolish as not having a plan at all. There will be times when you may have to punt, shift gears, adjust, shift on the fly, and listen to your natural instincts. There will be times that you should listen to others around you who may have a better way or better idea to accomplish the same goal, but first and foremost you need "A PLAN."

My eighteen-year-old son wants to be a major league baseball player. My sixteen-year- old son wants to be a famous singer and songwriter. As they get older their dreams and goals may change. They have learned at a young age, the importance of having a dream and the importance of investing their time into developing a solid plan. They have seen the positive results of following a plan as well as the negative results of neglecting the plan.

Let's say that today I'm pursuing a lifelong dream to dig a hole ten foot deep by ten feet wide and I have only a hand shovel with which to dig. My plan is to dig forty shovels of dirt per day for the next forty days. You see, I'm not sure that it will take forty days to complete this project. I think I'm close at 1600 shovels. Maybe I'm way off, I don't know, I've never dug a ten foot deep by ten foot wide hole. But I'm going to find out how long it takes because I'm going to stick to my plan. Now, maybe I'll realize that I can easily do eighty shovels per day and maybe I finish in twenty days. I won't know until I try. Once you have explored your obstacles you can begin to formulate a plan to overcome each one.

As you begin to develop your own plan, it is vital and prudent to explore the risk/reward factor. In other words, what are you sacrificing in order to accomplish your goals and is the sacrifice worth the outcome? Sacrifice usually includes family, health, time, financial security, and once again involves your dedication, perseverance, and courage to see the plan through. Having a balanced plan, that takes into account all of these factors, will more times than not, be the plan that prevails and can legitimately be called, "successful". You can have a detailed plan to open a restaurant and have all the pieces come together quickly as far as hitting your weekly gross revenue, profit margins, and waiting lines out the door. However, if you don't have a grip or a solid game plan on how to handle that success, you'll find yourself complaining and being miserable around the very ones you love, who sacrificed right along with you when you started your business. Knowing this can happen, and often does, your initial plan that specified taking the proper time to be with your family, hiring the right people, and spending your money and time wisely so you can grow your business, is the only game plan that will ever make sense. Learning to delegate to others and manage your time wisely is key to any successful venture. It's awesome to dream big, but never loose sight that a plan filled with wisdom is the key component to take your dream to places that few have ever ventured. Plan today, and your hopes and dreams for tomorrow will be far more rewarding when you wake up one day and realize you're in the midst of living your dream.

Chapter Five

Tiptoe through the Tulips &... Onions?

"Failure is the only way to begin again, more intelligently."
                    Henry Ford

During the following spring, my dad suggested that we sell flowers on Easter weekend, Mother's Day weekend, and Memorial Day. Flowers were another one of his passions in life, along with fruits and vegetables. In the late winter months of February and early March, I went with my dad to a wholesale flower grower just over the border in Connecticut. It was there that we walked through several one-hundred-foot-long greenhouses loaded with tulips, hyacinths, daffodils and various other flowers that were still a month or so away from blooming. Within a few minutes of arriving Dad began negotiating a deal. "Now, Mike," he started out, as if he were best friends with this guy and knew him for thirty years, "Are you sure these tulips are going to be popping by Easter?"

Mike quickly replied, "Yes, Mr. Olerio, I promise, they'll be in full bloom."

My dad then looked him in the eye and firmly asked, "How much you asking per pot?"

Mike quickly replied, "I need to get two dollars each."

My dad looked around for a moment and then shot right back with authority in his voice, "Shave a half a buck off the price of each pot and we'll take the whole greenhouse."

While Mike went into deep thought, pacing up and down looking at his magnificent crop of young tulips. I whispered to my dad in a sort of disbelieving urgent tone, "Dad, what are you thinking about here? There are over eight hundred pots of tulips in this greenhouse. We'll never sell all these plants in three days, this is crazy."

MELLOW PEACHES, THREE POUNDS FOR A DOLLAR

Like a man possessed with a passion, he gently pushed me aside, as if I were invisible and never said a word to him and walked up to Mike and said, "Are you sure these are going to pop by Easter?"

"Yes, I'm sure," said Mike, still in deep thought, half dazed from being caught off guard by my dad's proposal, "How about a quarter off each pot, Mr. Olerio?"

Without skipping a beat my dad stuck out his hand to shake and said, "$1.75 each, DONE. We need you to deliver them on the Thursday before Easter. How much deposit do you need?"

The second we got in the car, my dad looked at me with a huge childlike grin and said," I knew he would never take the half buck off; I would have taken the whole greenhouse for two dollars a pot. What a score, we caught him napping; man did we catch him napping! I hope they pop by Easter!"

I just stared straight ahead through the windshield and thought to myself, "What did he just get me into, over here?"

We found a great spot to sell our flowers, a vacant roadside lot in a very congested area with plenty of slow-moving traffic. We rented an actual trailer, the type hauled by an eighteen-wheeler. We used it as our storage bin for the more than two- thousand pots of flowers we purchased. Besides the eight hundred pots of tulips, we went down to The Market and my dad bought an additional twelve hundred assorted flower pots, a mixture of mums, hyacinths and Easter lilies. As we had done so often in our green Ford truck, we filled these trailers to maximum capacity. My dad taught me well that displaying and merchandising are essential to selling any product. I could display with the best of them. I set up seven long tables straight across the lot close to the road, then using the flower packing boxes; I made a three tier pyramid-shaped display so it looked like one long, massive display of color.

The tulips were our lead item. Our homemade, extra-large, eight-foot-high wooden "A" framed sign, let everyone know that we had the best prices in town.

"Tulips $2.99," jumped out at every driver who rode by and was the bargain sale that made people flock to us in droves. Just like our mellow peaches, three pounds for a dollar, the tulips brought people in to buy the other more profitable flowers such as mums and hyacinths. Needless to say, we not only sold out all eight hundred tulips and all twelve hundred other assorted pots, but were scrambling on Easter morning trying to buy more.

Although my father had little more than a sixth-grade education, he had more savvy and street smarts than most Harvard business graduates. He could negotiate, he had the guts to buy and take a good calculated risk. He knew how to merchandise. He knew how to motivate, instill perseverance and encourage a strong work ethic. He knew that an investment of time was needed to be successful. He knew how to pull people in with bargains and make higher profit margins from other items. He knew that three pounds for a dollar and $2.99 was more appealing and effective than saying thirty-three cents per pound or three dollars each. He also knew that a big, colorful roadside sign was more effective than a smaller, lackluster sign. He also knew how to bail out if he made the wrong buy, to cut our losses and run, rather than NOT ADMIT you made a mistake and continue until it became disastrous. He knew, that customer service and a broad smile went a long way, and that a stern look right in the eye could intimidate the best of salesmen. It's these small tips of the trade and lessons learned that eventually led us to move mountains.

By the summer of 1974, I was ready as ever to start my summer peddling job. My brother decided to work near the university for the summer. With a new set of college buddies and a new girlfriend, peddling was the last thing on his mind. I developed a six-day route that was unbeatable! I was working twelve-hour days, but didn't really think much about the hard work. I also learned to buy on my own and negotiate my own deals down at The Market. When I made a mistake I would cut and run. I soon learned that I had what it takes to be a good businessman. Oh yeah..., one more thing, I could yell, "Mellow peaches, three pounds for a dollar," every bit as well as my dad. At the end of the summer, I had socked away quite a nice chunk of money for a young man just graduating from high school.

I continue to share these stories, because I believe they set a stage for you, just as they did for me. When you set out and are preparing to accomplish great feats you need to carry the shield of wisdom in one hand and the sword of determination and persuasion in the other. It's just a part of the armor you will need to equip yourself for battle.

Unfortunately, I had some flaws that were beginning to surface and show their ugly head. I wasn't a good student. I didn't care much for school. I only did what I needed to get by. By September of 1974, I attended a junior college about five miles from home basically just to say I was going to college. The Vietnam War was over, so my fears of going to Vietnam had passed, but the flower power/hippie culture of the sixties had well planted its roots in society. Peace, love and rebellion had a foothold in my life. It was the dawning of the "Age of Aquarius," and I was searching to find out who I was. I transferred from the junior college, moved out of my home, and attended the University of Rhode Island as a non-matriculating student.

One great thing that came out of my URI experience was that I met the love of my life, a Jewish girl named Marjorie Weinstein. Being the type of guy who always knew what I wanted, I asked Margie to marry me within two weeks of our meeting. My wife maintains it was three weeks, even today, but I know it was definitely only two weeks.

From 1974 until the beginning of 1977, I had been on my own; I hadn't peddled and had long gone through every dollar that I had put in the bank. The one thing I still had was my 1962 green stake body Ford. It was Margie, her black dog and I in my '62 Ford truck. We wore shell necklaces around our necks. I wore ripped jeans and she wore flowered dresses. We were hippies, flat broke, and absolutely madly in love with each other. She accepted my marriage proposal and we both decided to move back to our homes in Cranston, Rhode Island, until we could scrape enough money together to marry and find an apartment to start our lives together. Although living together was beginning to become the accepted lifestyle, Margie and I both knew it was unacceptable in our families. Margie's dad and I immediately became friends. He knew how much I loved his daughter and was quite pleased that I asked for his permission to marry her.

Feeling the urgency now to show that I was a responsible young man, combined with the fact that I was flat broke, I needed to find a way to make some money. In the following winter months of 1977, I went down to The Market and worked on the loading docks unloading trucks. My dad knew I was floundering, but he also knew I was in love and that there was no stopping me from marrying Marjorie. We sat down together in the living room of my childhood home one early spring afternoon and had one of those heart- to-heart, father-and-son talks. He had just suffered from the first of many heart attacks, at age fifty-one, and didn't appear as strong looking as he had always been throughout his life. My hair was long, my jeans still torn. I had dropped out of college, had no money, no real job and no direction for my life. "You know," Dad started, "I can always try to get you into the post office as a mailman. It's a federal job, the pay is decent, you'll never get rich of course, but the benefits are good and you don't have to work real hard." It was just my father's way of getting under my skin. What he was really saying was, "You want anything in this life, you gotta sweat, you gotta grind, you gotta work twelve-hour days."

Within just a few days after our "post office" conversation I was staring out my bedroom widow at my green truck parked in the driveway when, all of a sudden, a light bulb went on in my head. I had an idea! I had a plan! I remember making a tight fist and shaking my arm back and forth while saying aloud to myself, "OH, YEAH!" It was a great idea that was staring me right in the face. It was this plan that eventually turned out to be one of the great success stories of my young life.

The very same Maria's Restaurant/banquet hall that I had worked in washing dishes as a kid had recently burned to the ground. After the cleanup, all that remained was one big parking lot. I made arrangements with the owners of the restaurant to rent a section of their vacant land for two hundred dollars per month on a month-to-month basis. I then told my dad my plan. He nodded his approval and I asked him to take a ride with me to The Market to look for some buys. We decided we would go with a "straight load" (just one item) to get a feel as to whether this plan was going to work. Dad hadn't lost his touch; he negotiated to buy a pallet of large Spanish onions that were packed in long wooden crates, about fifty pounds per crate. I loaded up my truck, which was starting to show her age, but could still handle a load of forty wooden crates weighing 2000 pounds. We headed for the vacant lot on Park Avenue in Cranston anxious to see if the plan would work.

With my "A" frame wooden sign from the flower days, a can of red spray paint and some stencils, I made two cardboard signs **ONIONS, 5lbs. For $1** and stapled them to each side of the A frame. I backed my truck close to the edge of the busy road and my dad and I proceeded to make one massive onion display on the back of the

MELLOW PEACHES, THREE POUNDS FOR A DOLLAR

truck.

What happened next absolutely blew our minds. One customer stopped, said, "I'll take ten pounds."

Another customer stopped, said, "Give me five pounds."

Then another, "Fifteen pounds, please."

Before we knew what was happening we were swarmed with people around our truck waiting in line to buy these onions. Some were old faithful customers that I had on my peddling routes, some were flower customers, but most were first-time buyers. Within three hours, forty crates containing 2000 pounds of onions were completely sold out. My dad and I just looked at each other in disbelief. We were laughing and shaking our heads in awe of what had just happened. We were like two little kids who had just received an inheritance of two years' supply of cotton candy. My dad kept saying over and over again, half out of breath, "I don't believe it, I don't believe it."

At the same time I kept repeating, "Did you see that? Did you see all those people? This spot is a goldmine."

Then we both looked at each other and were thinking the same thought at the same time. "Let's go back down to The Market and get some more onions."

I was back. I was ready to take on the world.

Chapter Six

Down With Gypsy Fruit Stands

"It is faith, and not reason, which impels men to action. Intelligence is content to point out the road but never drives us along."
                                         Dr. Alex Carrel

My dad and I proceeded to go back to The Market very early the next morning and buy more onions. After the brief negotiation ritual, we bought out the remaining seventy-two crates. I guess the salesman figured anyone that buys over one hundred crates of onions in two days deserves to haggle over saving an additional twenty-five cents per crate, so he gladly wrote the order. In addition to the onions, we purchased twenty boxes of peaches, twenty-five cases of cantaloupes, ten cases of bananas, and twenty burlap bags of sweet corn. Quite an impressive load, but after what we had just observed the day before we weren't too concerned. With my old faithful truck filled to capacity followed by a delivery truck carrying the remainder of the load, we proceeded back to our open air fruit stand, arriving on location at 7:30 a.m. We set up our outdoor market until it looked like a roadside farm in the middle of suburbia. We were ready for action. In addition to the onions being featured on our large "A" frame sign to attract the crowds, we hit them with the old standby **Mellow Peaches 3 lbs. for a Dollar,** in hopes to attract the crowds once again.

If we thought we were causing a scene the day before with people coming in droves to buy onions, the second day literally blew our minds. I had to recruit Margie, her girlfriend, and my two younger brothers because we just could not keep up with the crowds. Thirty to forty people at a time hovered around us like bears on honey, to buy our fresh produce at old-time bargain prices. By two in the afternoon, the frenzy was over! We were completely sold out!

Everything was happening so fast. We had to make some quick decisions and some necessary adjustments. First and foremost, we needed to keep our produce out of the hot sun if we were going to continue to buy in large quantities. We had to find a way to display our produce so we weren't selling off the back of the truck anymore. A health department official had stopped earlier that day to buy some peaches. He gave us a friendly warning to keep the produce off the ground. In the meantime, good ole' Dad was not only twenty-five years old again, but was basking in the glory of knowing that our new spot was the corner lot location that he always dreamed of, when he was a young man. This was it! We had hit the big time, and he knew it. At The Market, the word already spread like wildfire, up and down the walk, that the Olerios had struck gold on Park Avenue.

Without hesitating, I called Margie's Uncle Eddie. He ran a family business, an old-time supermarket called The Food Basket located in the heart of downtown Providence. They had been in business well before World War II. Uncle Eddie had heard about our oil strike on Park Avenue. Being an old produce man and veteran entrepreneur himself, he was eager and excited to help. I made three trips that evening back and forth from his market to our vacant lot with old display tables he used in the 1940's when they regularly mounded massive displays of produce on the sidewalks in front of their store. Uncle Eddy was proud to give me the display tables as he brought me up to the third floor of the old building, laughing and anxious to hear every detail about our newly discovered goldmine. With the assistance of a few of his employees, we wiped thirty-some years of dust off the tables and proceeded to carry them down three flights of stairs to my truck.

Family once again proved invaluable. The love of an old-time Jewish entrepreneur helping a young Italian/Catholic entrepreneur was significant. He made it quite clear I could rely on him for whatever was needed, to help the cause. He quickly recognized that I wasn't afraid of hard work and he knew I was madly in love with Margie. Nationality and religious differences were overshadowed by love and commitment to family.

While I was unloading Uncle Eddie's display tables, my dad journeyed off to three different department stores and cleaned them out of their entire patio umbrella inventory, fifteen in all. These would shade the produce that would otherwise wilt in the hot sun. Now the only problem we had was figuring out how to stand up the patio umbrellas and secure them from blowing away. That minor problem was quickly remedied as I made a late-night trip to Park Avenue Cement Company right down the road. They manufactured cinder blocks and just so happened to have square thirty-pound blocks with a hole right down the middle. I stacked four blocks one on top of the other and looked at my dad as we both smiled. They were absolutely perfect. By using a hand truck and sliding it under the four stacked cinder blocks we could easily move each stack from one side of the display tables to the other as the sun shifted during the day. We purchased sixty cinder blocks and arranged for an early-morning delivery. We went home and planned our strategy late into the evening hours to meet the demands of the next day's crowds. With a good solid plan and our adrenaline flowing we were ready to take on the world.

Morning came quickly! By 4:30 a.m. sharp, we were back at The Market. Joe Olerio didn't waste anytime letting everyone know he was the new "King of Produce." I could see it on his face and see it in his walk, which clearly suggested, "You want our business, then you better be willing to start shaving quarters and halves off the prices."

Our first purchase resembled the eight hundred tulip purchase from four years earlier and went like this:

"Carlo, what are you asking for cantaloupes this morning?"

Carlo quickly responded, "Four dollars a case, Joe."

My dad looked at the merchandise, put a cantaloupe up to his nose for inspection and responded, "How they eating?"

"Sweet as sugar, Joe."

My dad looked him in the eye and hit him with, "Give us two pallets (sixty cases), but I want them for $3.50."

With that Carlo quickly scurried into the office where the big boys hung out. We were at Tourtellot and Company, which just happened to be the largest produce house in Rhode Island and one of the largest wholesalers of peaches in New England. Irving Sigal, the company owner and president, stepped out of the office, walked up to Dad and me and said, "Joe, I'll give you the half a buck on the cantaloupes, as long as you buy all the peaches you'll need today from me. Give me the bulk of your business every day and I'll shave quarters and halves whenever I can."

My dad negotiated for 100 boxes of peaches (3800 lbs.), which were big time numbers.

That morning our reputation on "The Walk," reached legendary status. Crowds of old-timers, shipping clerks, and truck drivers watched in amazement at the amount of produce being loaded onto several delivery trucks to be shipped to our "Open Air Fruit Stand." Most wholesale owners who in the past never even gave me the time of day, were now eager to come up to me and shake hands as they lobbied for our business. Salesmen, on "The Walk," became our best friends. Our purchases started to reach supermarket chain levels. We also attracted the local farmers. They flocked to us as if it was the year 1780 and we were the only trading post for one-hundred-fifty miles. The farmers, hauling in their early-morning harvests, added just the right touch to the freshness and homespun feel of our open air market. From our humble beginnings of having our old faithful green '62 Ford truck sitting quietly on a vacant lot selling onions, we transformed our business into "THE OPEN AIR MARKET OF MARKETS." The sight was one for the ages. Thirty white display tables from the 1940s were strategically positioned throughout the lot, holding massive displays of fresh fruits and vegetables. Fifteen colorful patio umbrellas held up by cinder blocks were set in place to maximize every square inch of shade and could easily be seen by oncoming traffic five blocks away. Eight old-fashioned red and black hanging scales were conveniently dispersed and hung from makeshift two-by-four stands so that our sales clerks could work the crowds. Rows and rows of hand baskets and bushel baskets, of freshly picked vegetables, made a natural border around the entire fruit stand. I can only describe those days and weeks as the most intense of my young life. Each day became busier and crazier to a point of almost hysteria. Word of mouth traveled throughout the state about some wild open air fruit stand on Park Avenue.

We were a phenomenon, an honest-to-goodness success story. A young entrepreneur who once peddled produce through neighborhoods and sold flowers on the street corners hits the big time. We were a blast from the past and everyone wanted to be a part of it. It wasn't just the great buys and fresh fruits and vegetables; it was all about being part of something that made people believe, again, in the

American dream. Throughout the busy days, customer after customer would come up to me and say, "I drive all the way from Narragansett (30 miles away) to shop here."

"I drive all the way from Westerly (45 miles away)."

"I drive all the way from Smithfield."

"I love it here."

"I'd like to introduce you to my great-grandfather! He used to peddle with a pushcart up Federal Hill in the twenties and thirties."

By this time, the support staff needed to handle the crowd consisted of eleven of us working from sunup to 6 p.m. We only lifted our heads up to weigh produce on the hanging scales and only took individual breaks to shovel down a quick lunch and go to the bathroom. Our cash registers were our pockets! Our calculators were our pens and the customers' receipts were the brown paper bags that they stuffed chock full of produce. It was an old-time way of doing business and people embraced it with the same love and passion we put into it.

In our fourth week of business, the scene can only be described as pandemonium. A group of seven local fruit stand and grocery store owners got together, hired an attorney to represent them and went to the Cranston Chamber of Commerce to file a complaint claiming unfair competition because of the lack of overhead I had in the open air. Their argument was that their businesses were subjected to year-round expenses they incurred being indoors; why should we be allowed the benefit of setting up a summer business outside. They just couldn't compete with me. They also claimed I was selling produce that wasn't properly stored to meet local and state health standards because much of the produce was dropped off by the farmers in baskets and crates and stayed on the ground until we sold it. Funny thing was, nothing ever stayed on the ground very long.

My dad and I knew there was obvious tension between us and the local business owners. It didn't take a rocket scientist to notice every morning, on "The Walk," that these same business owners would snub their noses up at us or turn their heads away in disgust. Looking back, who could blame them. We were demolishing them, as if they were "Custer's Last Fruit Stand" and we were "The Italian Indians." We just never realized that it would get so severe, that they would form an alliance and hire a law firm to represent them, against us. Nevertheless, they came at us. So now, as far as my dad and I were concerned, it was all- out war. To add fuel to the fire, we purposely bought 100 cases of strawberries (1200 pints) and ran a special on our big sign: "FRESH STRAWBERRIES 2 PINTS FOR A DOLLAR." Working on only ten cents profit per pint, we made our statement loud and clear, "If you want to mess with us we're going to make you pay." We sold out every last pint within four hours.

To make matters worse, *The Cranston Mirror*, the city newspaper, came out with a front-page article including a picture of my fruit stand complete with umbrellas, truck, hanging scales and the droves of people shopping all huddled together like ants on flypaper. The headline read; "DOWN WITH GYPSY FRUIT STANDS." The article went on to explain the complaint being brought forth against the city of Cranston by the local businessmen regarding licensing issues, unfair competition, and health issues.

The day after the article was printed our business actually doubled. I was quickly becoming a believer that there was "no such thing as bad publicity." With that thought, I called the state's largest newspaper *The Providence Journal Bulletin*. It just so happened that a female reporter had just read the *Cranston Mirror* article and was anxious to take on the story. The following morning, with a *Journal Bulletin* photographer by her side, this young reporter gazed first hand at our wild open air gypsy fruit stand. Just as my dad spoke in disbelief on the first day we sold the onions, this reporter just kept repeating out loud, "I don't believe it! I can't believe what I'm seeing!" She observed the hundreds and hundreds of people pouring into our open air market as if the produce were free and we were giving them twenty dollar bills on top of it.

She asked me how I felt about the, "Down with Gypsy Fruit Stand" accusations, and how I felt about the other fruit stand owners. My response was quick and to the point. I said, "Free enterprise, isn't that the American way? I was always taught competition was good for business! I'm just working hard and building my business! Isn't that what the American dream is all about?"

The following morning one full page was devoted to my story with the amazing headlines; "Free Enterprise?" Whose Definition?" The story explained in detail the challenges that a young entrepreneur faced. She touched the hearts of the readers with quotes such as, "Twenty year old Matthew Olerio wakes up at 4:30 a.m. every morning and travels to the Providence Wholesale Market. He works hard and puts in long days that usually end around 8 p.m." She went on, to voice her own strong opinion, as well as my comments, on America's free enterprise system. It was an incredible story that displayed her overwhelming support for us and explained why she felt the fruit stand owners were fighting a losing battle. The article was accompanied by a photo of me with my green truck in the background surrounded by herds of frenzied shoppers. It also addressed a quote by the city councilman at large, who eventually went on to be mayor. As director of the city Chamber of Commerce, he introduced an ordinance that would prohibit roadside stands, unless they were operated by farmers on their own land. He also affirmed that he was only introducing the ordinance and had not decided whether he would support it or not, stating that, "I think Matt Olerio has some valid points…this is a free enterprise system."

When I arrived at The Market, early that morning, it seemed as if every owner, salesman, shipper and truck driver had read or was in the middle of reading, "the article." To this day, I cannot truly express what I was feeling, as I roamed "The Walk" as one person after another came up to me with a big smile, a pat on the back, a firm handshake and conversation that went something like this: "Way to go, Matt, don't back down! We're all behind you down here." You see, although the fruit stand owners who came out against me were steady customers to all the "wholesale houses," the story became bigger than life. "The Market" couldn't help but root for a twenty-year-old kid, who was taking on a slew of grown businessmen. This story that had all the makings of a "David and Goliath," Hollywood movie. This was a true, American success story in their eyes. I had their support and had won the hearts of the entire produce market, from the pompous owners, all the way down to the hardcore tough guys that worked the docks.

When I arrived back at my fruit stand, I had to squeeze and maneuver my truck through a wild mob scene as I watched and listened to my brothers and Margie desperately pleading with the crowd to stay back and allow them to set up. I jumped out of the truck and stood up right on the hood and yelled out as loudly as I possibly could, "Please, please, move back until we're finished setting up!"

I jumped from the truck and quickly motioned with my hands like a traffic cop working the rush hour traffic, as I led them back behind an imaginary line.

They all knew I was the kid in the newspaper article and they actually listened quite attentively to me. I could actually hear people in the crowd saying, "That's him, that's him, that's the young man in the newspaper."

I assured them that if they would allow us just forty-five minutes to set up, there would be plenty of produce for all. Not only did everyone stay, but the crowds continued to grow thicker. They watched these hard-working, enterprising entrepreneurs, who stood up for free enterprise, go through the morning ritual of the setup.

Local farmers pulled in with extra loads of vegetables already anticipating the frenzy from the newspaper article. Bill Stamps from Stamps Farm pulled in with seventy-five bags of sweet corn (375 dozen) and yelled to me over the crowd, "Matt, if you need more, call my wife and we'll try to have more picked for you and delivered by noontime."

The crowds were becoming so heavy that at one point Margie frantically latched onto my arm, looked at me as if the Hoover Dam was about to give way, and yelled in my ear in a panicked voice, "Matt, what are we going to do once you tell them it's ok to come in?"

There was a sense of panic in all of us, but at the same time there was an excitement level that was indescribable. My mom and dad had pulled into the lot and had somehow managed to push and weave their way through the crowd by telling people, "That's our son."

My parents had their own looks of concern and panic in their eyes, but were as excited as two little kids. My dad's usual standby lines all came out at once with his eyes bulging out of his head (again) as he was trying to speak to me over the loud humming buzz of the crowd. "What the hell is this? I don't believe it, I've never seen anything like it in my life."

I looked over at him, half exhausted from unloading and ripping open boxes like a wild man and running on pure adrenaline. I yelled out, "It's the newspaper article, Dad. It's the article." We looked at each other from a distance, shook our heads and smiled. We both knew at that moment in time, we were living the dream. We felt a tremendous sense of accomplishment, more than we ever had. We took on the entire state! We lived the dream! Holding on to that thought, I went up to the crowd, motioned with my arms in the air, and yelled out, "COME ON IN, THANKS FOR WAITING."

Your Five-Year Plan

It's time to write out your five-year plan. This plan needs to include your most ambitious goals and your greatest expectations. Be realistic to a point where you know the possibilities do exist for achieving them.

For example:

Saying that you want to obtain your PHD in the next eighteen months, and yet you have never attended college, just isn't logical. However, setting your goal to obtain your PHD in seven years can happen if that is truly your heart's desire and passion.

Your Five-Year Plan envisions yourself accomplishing seemingly impossible goals, but isn't a fool-hearted plan. Set your sights higher than you ever have, and start believing that you can reach them. Let the words "Go for it" take on a whole new meaning in your life.

We have already discussed the extreme importance of developing a solid plan. As you develop your ultimate five-year plan, be sure it isn't a plan that limits you to just a career and making money. It should be a plan that involves all the key aspects of your life including: spirituality, marriage, family/parenting, career, finances, community work, etc.

Reaching seemingly impossible goals will only be realized once you recognize that you need an unwavering commitment and a deliberate course of action to see them through. Take action on whatever you write down for your five-year plan. Be sure to include down time for hobbies. All work and no play can often be counterproductive. You need to reward yourself from time to time, especially when you're making great strides! So, include hobbies and other interests that will take your mind off your work. You'll find it to be refreshing and restful. It will improve your creativity and give you the needed energy and clear mind to keep forging ahead. Don't put your words on paper if you don't plan on having them jump off the page and turn into reality. Act on this plan as you have never acted on anything else in your lifetime and never stop believing.

Example:
Key Aspects of my life that I value: (in priority)
Prayer Time/Worship Time (Spiritual)
Spending quality time with my family (Relational)
Health and Fitness Time (Physical)
Stable income and savings (Financial)
Coaching & Music (Social)
Fishing/skiing/golf/hiking (Recreational)

In Five Years I want to:

Start my own company
Save $____ and pay off all my credit card/miscellaneous debt
Spend more quality time with my family
Purchase Oceanfront property
Run for Political office and win
Write a book and have it published

Key Aspects of my Life I value:

_____
_____

My Five-Year Plan:

_____
_____

Chapter Seven

Patio Umbrellas Never Die, They Just Turn Into Big, White Tents

"By their fruits ye shall be known..."
Matthew 7:20

As the crowds of people flocked to our open air market/gypsy fruit stand the numbers grew to almost uncontrollable levels. My dad and I had to regroup and think fast and hard. The first thing we did was purchase an enormous white tent that spanned forty feet in width by eighty feet in length. It was the kind of tent you might see at an outdoor wedding. We had it installed late one Saturday night, so we wouldn't lose a single day of business. Our colorful "Gypsy" umbrellas, that served their purpose so well, were now retired. When the crowds gazed upon our enormous tent on Monday morning, they embraced it with overwhelming approval. Other fruit stand owners attempted to combat it with their own plan of attack. Some of them began to make their own open-air displays in front of their stores. But it was to no avail. Our business wasn't just about fruit and produce anymore. By this time, it had transformed into something far beyond our wildest expectations. It was now like a high-speed locomotive train shifted into overdrive. There was just no stopping us!

With all the publicity surrounding our open air market, the conflict became a major political opportunity for many local politicians, who willingly expressed their opinion on the subject in various newspapers. A date was set for a major showdown at Cranston City Hall with the city council and Chamber of Commerce members deciding our fate. If the fruit stand business owners and their attorneys were to win, anyone who resembled a peddler, including the vendors with lemonade trucks, the ice cream man, the flower peddlers, and even the little old man selling hot dogs on the corner, from his stainless steel push cart, could be forever banned from conducting business in the city of Cranston, Rhode Island. That one fateful day of selling some onions on a corner, turned into an all-out political war that could change laws written two-hundred years earlier.

    I went to the nearby drug store and purchased a dozen sheets of the largest white poster board I could find. On the top of each sheet Margie wrote **STAND UP FOR FREE ENTERPRISE** in bold, black magic marker. For two weeks prior to the date of the great city hall showdown; almost every person who walked under our tent signed their John Hancock on Margie's posters in support of the American Dream. Literally thousands of signatures filled the back and front of these giant petitions, signatures of men, women, and children who believed in free enterprise. Thousands of signatures, accompanied by countless pats on the back and by massive purchases of fresh produce reaffirmed our fight. To show our gratitude I made a deal with Wesco Banana Company, one of only two wholesale houses in the state that dealt strictly with bananas. The deal was that they would deliver fifty cases of bananas a day (2000lbs.), at a reduced cost to me and I would run them as a solo lead item on my big "A" frame sign. Mellow Ripe Bananas 4 lbs. for a Dollar. If you think Mellow Peaches 3 lbs. for a Dollar made people go crazy, Bananas 4 lbs. for a Dollar sent people into a buying frenzy. Needless to say, there weren't too many bananas being sold anywhere else within a ten-mile radius of us, and that included the major supermarket chains; which by now were also feeling the effects of our madness in their own produce departments.

    There was excitement in the air all day long leading up to the night of the great battle at City Hall. Everyone was talking about it, from the guys hanging out at Sam the Barber's, to the daily lunch crowd of politicians, philosophers and intellectuals hanging out at Joe Pashalian's Boston Submarine Shop. It was the main topic of conversation in the city. It was like the anticipation leading up to the gunfight at O.K. Corral, when Wyatt Earp and Doc Holiday were about to ride into town.

    It was a beautiful and balmy night. The action unfolding in the second-floor auditorium at City Hall could only be described as a lynch mob courtroom scene. Men, women, and children were crammed into a large room like sardines. They were sweating, chattering and fanning themselves with homemade paper fans. On one side of the room, the fruit stand and grocery store owners sat with their families and their attorneys. On the other side was my Italian family, my soon to be Jewish in-laws, and my friends and customers. It resembled a huge Italian wedding, minus the cake and the band. When all the seats in the room were filled to capacity, the crowds overflowed in the rear, on the side isles, and out the doors into the halls.

The city council president banged his gavel frantically while attempting to call the meeting to order, yelling repeatedly, "I'll have order in this auditorium or I'll have the entire room cleared!"

After a brief introduction and briefing as to exactly why we were gathered on that evening, the proceedings began. First the lead attorney for the business owners began to plead their case. After staring at this man for a few minutes, my jaw dropped a good two inches. I realized that he was the man in the suit that I waited on during that morning at my fruit stand. He began his spiel, speaking like an Oxford man, delivering each word with an almost old English type of drawl, but using perfect diction. "I visited a certain open air fruit stand this morning and purchased four plums. The asking price per pound, for the plums, was thirty-nine cents. The total price charged to me for the plums after being weighed on a manual hanging scale was forty-two cents weighing in at slightly over one pound. I then took those same four plums (which he held up in a brown paper bag for everyone to examine) and I weighed them on a Hobart computerized scale based on the same thirty-nine cents per pound price. Surprisingly enough, the total price for the same four plums actually came in at thirty-nine cents. They weighed in at an even one pound, a three cent differential from what I was charged earlier in the day by the open air market," he accused.

Their opening attack and obvious game plan was to attempt to prove that we were cheating the public by using antiquated hanging scales and not state-of-the-art computerized scales. What happened next was pure Hollywood. Vincent Faye, one of the five council members and a practicing attorney, stood up and looked directly at the opposing attorney and quizzed, "Sir, how much time lapsed after your purchase at the open air fruit stand in question until you reweighed those same four plums on the Hobart computerized scale?"

The opposing attorney thought for a second and answered, "Approximately four hours."

Mr. Faye quickly asked his second question, "And where did you keep those plums during those four hours?"

With a slight stutter, the opposing attorney replied, "Ahh…, in my car."

Mr. Faye responded with a sly smile and a slight nod of his head, "In your car? In that brown paper bag? Sir, what was the high temperature of the day?"

The opposing attorney turned expressionless and responded, "Well, uh… I believe it was around ninety-five degrees."

Mr. Faye, looking and sounding like Perry Mason in his prime, unleashed a thirty-second barrage at the opposing attorney without skipping a beat and without taking a breath: "Exactly ninety-five degrees, sir, ninety-five degrees. Sir, don't you realize that plums are made up of a very high percentage of water and water evaporates in extreme heat! Of course they would weigh less, four hours later, sitting in that brown bag in your hot car. I'm surprised they didn't weigh in at three-quarters of a pound! I'm surprised those plums didn't turn into prunes. Maybe that certain open air fruit stand had better have their scales checked to make sure their not cheating themselves."

The crowd went into an uncontrollable laughing fit and started applauding. Even the families of the fruit stand owners couldn't help but show a slight grin. Little did anyone know that Vincent Faye was a steady customer of mine. He was also an admirer of hard-working young men and women and, a lover of fresh fruit. I just never realized how loyal a customer he was, until that evening.

As the night progressed, the opposition pounded away with the "lack of overhead" issue. They continued to complain about unfair competition, noting that I didn't have the same overhead and year-round expenses they incurred. They explained that their businesses were suffering during their prime season. Then they questioned health department issues related to produce being improperly stored on the ground, while their businesses were subject to follow the strict guidelines set forth by the state and local health departments.

When it was my turn, as I began to stand up, I felt a hand on my shoulder. The hand belonged to Nathan Canaan, the owner of the largest potato wholesale house in Rhode Island. He asked me if he could speak first, on my behalf. Now I knew I was one of his best customers that summer, with perhaps, the exception of the larger supermarket chains. But I never anticipated that a wholesaler, who also relied on the business of all seven business owners in the room that evening, would want to stick his neck out and speak in my favor. Nathan was also a longtime friend of the family and he appreciated my strong work ethic, as much as anyone. His speech sent chills down the spines of the opposition. He began by staring directly at the business owners as if he had zero tolerance for what they were doing. "I can't believe what I am hearing tonight! Grown businessmen are going up against a twenty-year-old kid, just because he came up with a better idea than any of you. You talk about competition! Hey, just look at The Market! Wholesale houses are side by side! They've been competing and surviving since the late 1920s. Just like The Market attracts large crowds and creates the competitive spirit for our businesses, Matt Olerio is bringing thousands of people into Cranston to shop that would never otherwise be there. Why don't you each find a way to take advantage of that! Come up with your own creative ways to improve your businesses? And, as for the baloney, regarding health standards violations, and bushel baskets and boxes of produce placed on the ground, let's discuss the real health issues."

Nathan then turned and looked directly at the ringleader of the business owners who started the whole opposition group, who also just happened to be the largest restaurant/hospital wholesaler of lettuce and coleslaw in Rhode Island, and said, "John, you, of all people, bringing up health issues, when you deal with more iceberg lettuce and cabbage than any of us in this room. Let's not kid each other! We all know about the ongoing problem with migrant workers in the lettuce fields in California, where the nearest bathroom facilities are hundreds of acres away! Now, that's a health issue and concern." With that line, the crowd let out a loud gasp! Then Nathan concluded, "Matt Olerio, putting bushel baskets of produce on the pavement, is not creating a health issue. I've seen his operation. He's selling produce so fast, nothing ever stays on the ground long enough to even warrant a health concern. I think, more than anything, you're all jealous of what he has going for him and you don't know how to stop him. Keep up the good work, Matt!"

Nathan stepped down off the podium and the crowd erupted into a roaring round of applause. He had made his point loud and clear. They were barking up the wrong tree on the health hazard issue. He made the crowd believe in the cause for free enterprise and competition, more than ever, with his heartfelt speech and overwhelming show of support.

While the crowd was still cheering, my oldest brother Buddy, appeared from out of nowhere, and stepped up to the podium. I guess he figured that if anyone was going to mess with his kid brother, they were going to have to go through him first. Buddy had made his own mark in the city and state as a highly successful, respected businessman. He was also in tight with many local and state politicians. He wasted no time and immediately laid into the Cranston Chamber of Commerce members for even allowing such a fiasco to take place.

He adamantly pointed out, "Without a free enterprise system, many of you in attendance tonight would never have had the opportunity to be in business for yourselves."

I was extremely proud of my brother, as he stepped off the podium to an equally rousing applause. I remember thinking to myself, "Wow! What an overwhelming show of support, this is amazing, this is way beyond what I expected!"

My father also spoke that evening. I had often heard him yell and sell before, but never had I heard him speak in an open forum. I was extremely proud to be his son as he spoke calmly and eloquently about the freedom to start our own business, to work hard and realize the American Dream. He spoke about his parents coming to America, at the turn of the century, as Italian immigrants. He reminded many in the room that they had similar backgrounds. "The struggles and hardships our parents endured: living together in tenement houses, cold-water flats, five or six families all striving and pulling together to better themselves. They pooled their money together for food and rent until one by one they were able to get a place of their own and raise their families. This should not be forgotten. When you make an argument against free enterprise and competition and try to justify it, claiming you can't compete because of overhead, you're going against the same business principles most of your own parents used to better themselves and raise their families. You take away the competitive spirit in America, and you take away free enterprise. Then, you take away the very things that make our nation so great. My son isn't your enemy! He's working twelve to fourteen hour days and earning an honest living. He didn't reinvent the wheel. He went back in time, and used old business principles. The customers love it."

As my dad stepped down off the podium, the crowd again erupted into applause followed by a standing ovation, complete with high-decibel whistlers. The older Italian immigrants in the crowd, both men and women, had tears flowing down their cheeks as they stood up and cheered.

I really didn't know what else I could say after my dad's heart-wrenching speech. I went forward to the podium carrying the twelve white poster board petitions filled from top to bottom with customers' signatures. There at the top of each poster board were the words in bold magic marker that Margie had written, "Stand Up For Free Enterprise." The crowd became very still and very quite. Other than screaming out bargains in front of my customers, I wasn't used to public speaking, in front of such a large crowd. The sudden silence made me even more nervous. But I knew my family and friends were there for me, so I wasn't about to wimp out on them. I started to hold up each poster board one at a time, with my arms stretched high over my head showing the thousands and thousands of signatures sprawled across the sheets. I began to speak, "THIS IS WHAT THE PEOPLE OF RHODE ISLAND AND OUR OWN CITY OF CRANSTON HAVE TO SAY ABOUT FREE ENTERPRISE, AND REALIZING THE AMERICAN DREAM."

With that the place erupted into an all-out frenzy, clapping, banging on chairs, screaming, howling, and whistling. It was a spectacular sight that spoke volumes to the city council and fruit stand owners. In the meantime the city council president kept to his word given earlier. With gavel in hand, slamming down like a jackhammer, he ordered everyone to clear the room, for a fifteen-minute recess.

While we were in the halls, the crowds still buzzed with excitement. My grandma, who was eighty years old at the time, went up to one of the opposing fruit stand owners. All of a sudden, she went from a frail, elderly woman to a frisky twenty-year-old tiger. She lashed out at one of the fruit stand owners that she had recognized. In her half Italian, half broken English voice, with her finger pointing in his face, and venom in her words, she voiced her displeasure, "YOU..., how-a-did-a-you-a getta your start? I- a- rememba-you-a when-a-you-a were just a little a boy and you helpa your father up a Federal Hill. I use to buy fruit from-a-your-a father from the-push-a-cart." Just then her pocket book swung in the air as his arms went up over his face to defend himself. A circle of approximately thirty people were watching this scene. A few of us immediately stepped in, to hold my grandmother back and help her get control. But she continued, "What-a-did-a-my-a-grandson ever-a-do-a- to you? Tell-a-me, what-a- did-he ever do-a-to you?"

It was a memorable night, to say the least. We returned to the auditorium to a unanimous decision by the city council, to allow us to continue to sell fruits and vegetables. What they did approve was licensing requirements for all vendors selling in temporary locations. It was written into the city charter and stands to this day. It was an amazing victory for me, my family, my friends and customers. It taught me to never be afraid to stand up for what I believe. It taught me that there is strength in numbers. It showed me, once again that family, my future wife by my side, and loyal friends mattered to me greatly. They were key elements to my success.

Chapter Eight

The Dream Is Over...Yeah, Right!

"Two roads diverged in the woods, and I...I took the one less traveled by, and that has made all the difference."
                                        Robert Frost

Soon after realizing the plot of land that I was renting for my open air market, was a diamond in the rough, the owners confronted me and offered me the first opportunity to buy the lot, before they put it up for sale. Their asking price was fifty-three-thousand dollars, for prime real estate that spanned 80' x 200'. It was situated on a congested, slow moving traffic thoroughfare in one of the premier cities and locations in Rhode Island. My dad's response to their offer was, "What are they nuts or something! It's not worth more than forty-five thousand, and I won't pay them a penny more."

For days I kept at it. I knew money was tight for my father, after raising seven children. I knew his health concerns were in the forefront of his mind, so I kept repeating, "Dad, I can easily pay this land off within three years. I don't care if they're asking more than the going price for real estate! To me, it's worth every penny and more." When I realized he couldn't do it, I went to outside family members and begged, but to no avail. I walked into two banks and pleaded for a land loan but I was politely turned down. I asked the land owners if they would carry the note at a fair interest rate. Their response was, "Sorry, Matt, this land's a hot commodity now and we appreciate what you did to make it that way, but we need the money now, and we know we can get it."

If you were to ask my dad today, what his top three regrets are in his life, he will surely answer, as one of the three, that "I didn't buy my son the land on Park Avenue." It was the greatest buy in the world, our very own "gold mine." We could have put nails in brown paper bags and put out a sign: Rusty Nails 3 lbs. for a Dollar, and people would have stopped and bought them.

The land sold after the summer of 1978 ended. The great stand-off at city hall was now just a fond memory to look back on. It sold for the full asking price of fifty-three thousand dollars. I was devastated, but the one bright light was that there were no immediate plans for construction on the land and I was allowed to return again the following summer. The rent was raised to five hundred dollars per month, but I didn't care. At the same time, my brother, who used to quahog with me, decided he would join me in purchasing an indoor fruit stand approximately seven miles away from my gold mine spot. The prior owners just didn't understand the nature of the business and were failing miserably. When I closed the summer market, I went into business with Al. For me it was a challenge and it kept me in the produce business. By then, Margie and I had married and were in our own tenement apartment. My brother Al also had married. Now, we had a quartet working in our new endeavor. I went, from making the kind of money I was bringing in on Park Avenue, to having an inside store in a less ethnic area of the city, selling not only fruits and vegetables, but also milk, eggs, frozen foods, bread and canned goods, with a weekly paycheck of exactly $106. This was not my idea of forging ahead. I felt as if I had taken twelve steps and eight years backwards, and was at Maria's Restaurant again, washing dishes and listening to, "My Way" sung by the Frank Sinatra wannabe. Only this time, the words "Regrets, I have a few," took on a new meaning for me.

Don't get me wrong, we were extremely busy, but it took four times the amount of people, to do the same volume that I was doing on Park Avenue. Although we had many faithful customers follow us to our new indoor stand, we lost our appeal to generate the frenzied mobs, when we filled big brown bags with produce as though it was the end of the world and we were the only place on planet earth, with food. It just wasn't the same. To make matters worse, my brother totally hated the business. So much so, that after two years of agony, he started making serious plans to go into the restaurant business. I didn't blame him! We weren't a fruit stand anymore; we were a grocery store. Plus, our take-home pay took its toll on both of us, especially for the number of hours we put in and the bull work involved in the day-to-day operations. After coming to the reality that this wasn't our life- long career dream, we sold the business, got all of our money back and were even able to pay back our father, who had generously let us borrow $7,000.00 to get started. But always in the back of my mind was the thought of the missed opportunity in not buying the land back on Park Avenue.

How many times in your life have you heard this line, or even said it yourself: "I could have bought that land for $3,000.00, thirty years ago! Now look at it! It's worth a fortune today." Or... "I had a chance to buy this whole tract of land in the sixties for a song, now it's worth millions of dollars." Or perhaps, "If I only had the money, what I could have done forty years ago." I'm quite sure you've also heard the expression, "Would have, should have, could have." Well, guess what? Someone did buy that piece of land you were looking at for $3,000.00. They made a fortune because they did it! They did, what you were only thinking of doing. They took action on the same vision you wanted to act on. They took the risk. Yes, they had the $3,000 to buy the land when maybe you didn't, but let's not use the, lack of capital, as an excuse. The truth is; we tend to run scared at times when we should be charging ahead. We use the money excuse, which is somewhat valid, but not the true reason for our lack of stepping out and taking a good, calculated risk. Looking back, if I knew what I know today, I would have given the owners a down payment on the land to hold them off and spent every hour of every day trying to come up with a way to finance it! One way or the other, I would have found a way to buy that land.

I remember one night; an old friend of mine came to my home. He was a bit distraught and needed to talk. He had lost his job six months earlier; just two months after he and his new bride had just purchased a new home. He did manage to find another job, but the pay was substantially lower than his prior job. He looked at me as if his world was coming to an end. He said, "Matt, I put the house up for sale with a realtor yesterday. I went to a financial advisor and we just can't meet our monthly expenses. I'm short by more than four hundred dollars a month, and that's without us going out to dinner or any other miscellaneous expenses. I just can't make it work."

I asked him, "Do you have any money socked away in the bank or in a 401k, anything at all?"

He responded, "Well, I have my 401k rollover from my past job that has $325,000 in it! But that's for the future! That's our retirement security."

In total disbelief, I put my face right up to his and said, "Bill, this is your third marriage, right?"

He nodded yes.

"And you love this girl a whole lot, don't you?"

Again he nodded yes.

I immediately responded, "Well, be prepared to spend your retirement alone! If you sell this home, and she knows that you are sitting with $325K in a 401k plan, you might as well start packing tomorrow, because you're about to go three for three." Then I looked at him like an Italian who has lost his patience and yelled, "For goodness sakes, borrow against the 401k! Pay the penalties and use a portion of it to get you by, for one year or so, until a better job comes along. Let me tell you something, my friend. Do this now or you can plan on spending your retirement years alone with your dog and your 401k money, driving a Winnebago across country wondering what went wrong in your life."

I'm not exaggerating one bit! He left my home in less than two minutes, after I spoke those words! He drove to his home, pulled the For Sale sign out of the ground, threw it in the garage, went back inside and in front of his wife, picked up the phone, called the real estate agent and said, "We've changed our minds."

I ran into this lovely couple almost one year later and I got a warm hug from her and a firm handshake and big smile from him. He put the plan into action, kept his home and eventually did end up finding a better paying job. The real estate market had also changed for the better, which made his property value significantly increase.

Now I know that's an extreme story, but nevertheless a true one. It just goes to show us, how blind we can sometimes be, when it comes to taking a good, sound, calculated risk for something we believe in, such as the $3,000 that couldn't be found to buy the land deal of the century. In most cases, it's not that we couldn't find the money, it's more that we really didn't put our heart and soul into trying. We didn't explore and exhaust every last possibility, even if it meant borrowing the money at a higher than average interest rate from a friend or relative. The old adage is usually true, "Where there's a will, there's a way." We miss opportunities because we're not committed to the cause or we look at all the negatives instead of the endless possibilities.

Have there been times in my life where I've taken risks when I shouldn't have? You bet there have. I've taken risks to a fault many times and have paid dearly for it, both financially and emotionally. At age forty-seven, I've learned to curtail risks to be wiser, more calculated in risk/reward situations. But still, to not take the risk and never have tried is far more debilitating than going for it, and failing. It's the risk taker, who rises to meet seemingly insurmountable odds and accepts the challenges they bring and pushes through the obstacles, to face another day. It's the risk taker, who finds his/her dream because he or she didn't let the sheer thought of the risk overtake their mind and say, "Forget it; it's just too risky."

Just remember this about risk. It comes in many shapes and sizes. While many of us were still buying the NASDAQ at the 5,000 level in the year 2000 and taking that investment risk, there were traders shorting the market (banking on it to go down) and they made astronomical profits in the very same tech and telecom stocks that crippled those of us who went "long the market" (speculating they will go higher). So when people say to you that the market is just too risky, remember this. There are two ways to play the risk, or rather to invest in the risk. It's all in how you approach the situation and see where the opportunity lies. One man's opportunity could be another man's calamity. You can sail a boat into rough seas, capsize and drown or you can sail a boat into rough seas and win the World Cup.

After we sold our grocery business, we knew we needed a change. We were young and willing to take a risk.

We changed gears. We did a 180. My brother opened an extremely successful restaurant that became an overnight sensation. Of all places, it just happened to be in the same spot as the original Maria's Restaurant and right next door to my open air fruit stand on Park Avenue. When a three-store strip plaza was completed on the land, my brother was smart enough to seize the opportunity, and rented the end building with the most parking spaces. In the meantime, I went back to my vacant lot next door and made one last summer's attempt at what I knew best. Margie and I had our own plans and I needed to make as much money as possible to get us started. The crowds absolutely loved having us back and I loved being there again. But it would be my last time, in my young life to be a fruit and produce man. I was just turning twenty-four years old that summer. I was far from ever thinking that it was time to call it quits as an entrepreneur. We were getting ready for a new adventure. It was different than anything else our family had ventured into or was accustomed to, because it didn't involve food or selling insurance.

When I told my dad about my new career change, he was devastated. I remember his exact words as if they were said yesterday: "You're a natural for this business. You became an even better produce buyer than I. To walk away now, would be an absolute shame."

I looked at him and said, "Dad, I've got to try this while I'm still young. I know you don't want to hear this, but I've got to try."

My dad's dream was over, and my new dream. . . or shall I say Margie's dream, was about to begin.

Quite the impressive produce display at Olerio's Market

Leaps of Faith and Steps of Action

How do we become individuals that define resiliency, that never stop believing, that exemplify the "I will not quit, persona?"

1. Believe that positive change can come about in your life.

2. Take steps of faith, specifically toward those positive changes. If you are lacking faith, ask God to increase your faith, and ask Him to open doors that no man can shut.

3. Take action: physical, mental, and spiritual.

You also need to recognize that through these leaps of faith and steps of action, everything isn't always going to go according to your plan. Some things happen for a reason! Days that I initially perceived as major set backs in pursuing my dreams, often resulted in major victories, weeks, months, and even years later. Once you realize that every battle will not be won, and once you learn to recognize in yourself the "I will not quit persona," you'll get over the lost battles quickly and go on to win the next one and the one after that. In my humble opinion, those who never lose faith in God, in their dream, or in themselves, will be the individuals that press on to victory and see their dreams become reality.

I was taught the following serenity prayer when I was a young man and I often refer to it when I'm in my planning mode. "Lord, help me to change the things I can, to recognize those things that I cannot change and give me the wisdom to know the difference." (St. Francis of Assisi)

Chapter Nine

From Bananas to Drumsticks

"Sometimes we have the dream but we are not ourselves ready for the dream. We have to grow to meet it."
                                        Louis L'Amour

My employment experiences as a young man were centered on selling fruits and vegetables with my dad guiding and teaching me every step of the way. However, the little, flowered-dress girl, who became my wife and worked side by side with me selling fruits and vegetables, had a dream of her own. Margie could sing. Margie's voice is in the elite group category of superstar female vocalist in the country. Her entire Jewish family was blessed with talent as either childhood musical prodigies or professional ballet dancers. Margie's voice was powerful! Out of her petite 5' 1" frame came a radiant sound that would turn the heads of even the top singers in the world. With her voice, she never needed to take a back seat to anyone. For our new dream to unfold, there were two more pieces to this musical career puzzle. They consisted of my sister, Debbie and her husband, Lou, who just happened to be musical geniuses and very talented songwriters, trying to hit the big-time out in Los Angeles. I had played drums in a couple of rock bands during my teens, but it had been such a long time since I picked up a pair of sticks. I couldn't honestly call myself a legitimate drummer anymore. Debbie and Lou felt that their songwriting, combined with Margie's voice, were just the right ingredients to make a legitimate run at landing a record deal with one of the major labels. They knew that I was just crazy enough to give it a shot.

When I told my dad that I was about to embark on a new venture in music, his initial remarks were, "Do you realize how difficult it is to make it in the music business? It's not just having talent! It's being in the right place at the right time. It's having the right connections! It's a tough racket, one you know nothing about. Stick to what you know best. Don't make a mistake that you're going to regret for the rest of your life."

My dad had such a way with words! Deep down in my gut, I actually felt that he could be right, but at the same time, there was something burning inside of me that just kept saying, "Go for it while you're still young. Go for it, Matt!" And go for it we did.

For me, these were somewhat difficult times. I sold my old faithful green truck. That was one sad day. Many memories swept through my mind, as I was remembering all of the heavy loads she had carried and the many valuable lessons that I learned while she was part of my life. I was trading in my bananas for drumsticks! The thrill of being "King of Produce" was over.

I was pursuing a dream that wasn't really mine, not that my wife had to twist my arm or anything, I always wanted to do something adventurous such as play original music in a rock band and try to land a recording contract with a major record label. It's just that, while I believed Margie, my sister and my brother-in-law had the talent and desire to make it, I wasn't so sure about myself. I could hold a somewhat steady beat. I had plenty of rhythm and a good feel for drumming. But, I wasn't at the level that I needed to be, to go all the way, and I knew it. We practiced four to six hours per day seven days a week. When the band wasn't practicing, I was in the studio by myself practicing at least three hours a day. I started taking lessons from two of the best drum teachers I could find in Rhode Island. One was a rock drummer. I met with him twice a week. The other was a well-known jazz drummer. I worked with him once per week. I wanted to learn everything there was to learn about drumming. I became totally consumed with it. While Rhode Island's own Vinny Pazienza was training to be the welterweight champion of the world right down the road from me at his own gym, I was training to be an eighties version of Ringo Starr in my own studio. For one year straight I ate, drank, and slept drumming. It was all about the "grind" my father had taught me when I was a teenager. I practiced so much, I was bordering the fanatical. But my fears of inadequacy were slowly starting to subside. I was starting to believe that we were good enough to make it as a band. My drumming didn't have to take a back seat to anyone, because our practice and commitment had brought all of us to a new level. After six intense months of practicing together as a band, we were ready to try things out on the local music scene. We were able to book a gig at one of the hottest clubs in the Providence night scene.

We debuted on a Thursday night in the summer of 1980, at the underground club called The Living Room, located in an obscure spot in downtown Providence, Rhode Island. If you were a part of the "original music scene" in Rhode Island and Boston, you played "The Living Room." We were very well received by the mixed underground crowd of orange, Mohawk hair, ringed-nosed nocturnals, black leather and lace divas, gays and straight alike. We also had an avant-garde clique of college students from wealthy families who attended Rhode Island School of Design and Brown University. It was a far cry from selling "Mellow Peaches," but there was an excitement about it that intrigued me.

We soon booked our second gig. This time it was at Lupo's Heartbreak Hotel. This was an equally popular underground club that attracted as much of a wild and mixed crowd as The Living Room. They often brought in more well-known national recording acts from all over the country.

Once again, our music and style were very well received. An immediate buzz started around the city about a new high energy band, "Hi-Beams," that featured two hot-looking girls out front.

In the following six months of continuous bookings, nonstop rehearsals, and a constantly growing fan base, we decided that it was time to go into the recording studio and release a "45." We recorded at a state-of-the-art, twenty-four-track studio called, Normandy Sound, in Warren, Rhode Island. We requested the legendary Phil Greene to produce and engineer our first single. Phil Greene was eccentric, even bizarre at times. But, he was a great guy who happened to be a recording and musical genius. He was brash, if he thought that we could play it or sing it better, he held nothing back. He pushed us to realize every last bit of talent we had in our bodies. After three very intense, very expensive weeks in the studio, we released our first record. The title cut, a high-energy pop song called "Hyperactive," was on the "A" side and a controversial avant-garde, "White People" was recorded on the "B" side. "White People" was actually anti-apartheid, but its title sometimes sent the wrong message. When the semiannual music reviews came out in *The Newpaper*, the final and most respected word on original music in Rhode Island, "Hyperactive" literally, stole the show. Newpaper music writer, Bob Angell, wrote, "Aha! Here's a good 'un. Commercial, punchy, not too new wavey. Sparking pop with female vocal lead. This bright, light quartet, it is now apparent, will escape the death throes of the local new wave scene and continue to flourish largely on the strength of this new debut single. A strong entry. Dig it, only ten years ago, local groups struggled to catch up with radio standards. Now, the tables have turned. When will commercial radio catch up with today's locally produced music?"

Rhode Island's number-one alternative rock station, "WBRU," immediately embraced "Hyperactive!" They actually put it on their regular song rotation, alongside their national recording artists. Hi-Beams and "Hyperactive" were hotter than hot, and there was no stopping us. It was 1981 and suddenly, we were all over the air waves in Rhode Island, Boston, and New York. We even mysteriously ended up receiving air play in Germany on several underground radio stations. After playing for almost two years in every dive from New York to Boston, we were finally starting to be recognized as one of the top new bands in New England. Our shows became wilder, attracting huge crowds. By this time, "Hyperactive" was a smash local hit and our audiences would literally break into an all-out wild and bizarre frenzy that made the crowds on Park Avenue buying bananas, four pounds for a dollar, look like a picnic in the park.

I will never forget when a predominately gay club hired us to kick off their "opening night," gala blast, dance party. They paid us well and the place was absolutely jam packed with people. Hundreds of gays and straights alike jammed and packed into this new, hot, dance club like sardines in a can. I knew my life was drastically changing! During one of our songs, as I was pounding away on my drums, I looked over to my left and then to my right, and then to my left again and again to my right as I watched in disbelief while two giant, human-size bird cages came rising up from out of the floor surrounded by white smoke. Two guys emerged, inside the cage, dressed in drag, dancing away, shaking their heads and hips to our music, as if they were Go-Go girls from the 60s. Margie turned to me as she was singing, and our eyes met through all the hysteria and clouds of smoke. The look in her eyes said it all. We both knew we weren't in Kansas anymore; and we certainly weren't in our green truck selling peaches, either.

Everything moved into overdrive. *The Providence Journal* newspaper got in on the act, as music critics were hyping us as the "band on the verge." Those articles were followed by several interviews with, both, mainstream and underground radio stations, as well as college campus newspapers and radio stations. By this time, "Hyperactive" was receiving equal playing time with songs by prominent bands such as: the Police and U2. Our 45, recorded under our own label, "New Breed Records," was literally flying off the shelves in New England.

While all this was taking place, I felt so unsettled. I just wasn't happy. For months I'd been telling Margie that this lifestyle isn't for us. I longed to open up boxes of peaches, or peppers or cantaloupes and just stack them up into beautiful displays. I told her "I'm not cut out for the rock'n'roll lifestyle," which by now was starting to take its toll on me physically. I had lost quite a bit of weight. I was pale, drawn and tired. In the fruit and produce business, I would leave for work at 4:30 AM, but in this new career we weren't going to bed until then. Yet, Margie urged me to keep going! She could taste success! She could see her dream unfolding before her eyes and she would say, "Look how far we've come in such a short time, we can't stop now."

Two major events took place for us in the spring of 1983 that dramatically changed our direction and brought us to another level. First, "The Probers," who were recognized as another very hot band on "the verge" in Providence, were asked to do a show with us at the very prestigious "Center Stage" night club/concert hall. The only glitch was, we had to be the opening act and The Probers would be the headliners. At first, we declined because we felt that the show should have been booked with us headlining. We knew we could outdraw them three to one by this time in our careers. But after careful consideration, and realizing that a lot of politics were involved, we reluctantly agreed. It was a great place to be seen, and besides, the band U2, which was really starting to heat up in America, was scheduled to play there on the night before us. It was a good weekend to be playing in Providence.

The big night came! We were told we would take stage at the very early time of 9:00 p.m. That made us even more upset because the nightlife didn't explode until around midnight, when most of the nocturnals and groupies came out. We took the stage right at nine and all of a sudden, I thought I was back selling peaches three pounds for a dollar on Park Avenue. Right before our eyes, hundreds and hundreds of fans poured into this place and for the next hour and a half they went absolutely wild over us. After two encores we left the stage and went back to our dressing rooms in absolute shock. We knew that we were growing in popularity. But we never expected that we could fill a place like Center Stage at 9:00 p.m., as an opening act. What happened in the next half-hour blew our minds. When The Probers took the stage at midnight more than half the place cleared out. There was no denying who the crowd came out to see and hear. We proved that we could draw fans, and we had a following that other bands in the area envied.

The second major event occurred when we were invited to enter the WBCN Rock Rumble. WBCN was Boston's hottest station at the time. Any national recording artist that played Boston couldn't avoid WBCN. They ruled the land! They held the major interviews and set the pace for rock, punk and anything else in between. "The Rumble" was one of their annual premier events that drew large numbers of original rock bands from all over New England to compete against each other. The winners and runner-up were awarded recording time at The Cars', a recording studio in Boston, a shot to play in front of major record label executives, cash, musical instruments, and a whole lot of free air time. Every club manager, who meant anything to original music, attended "The Rumble." They would book the top bands instantly. We were basically told by everyone in Rhode Island, including newspaper critics and club owners, to just go and have a great time. They all mentioned the politics of the Boston music scene would never recognize or allow a Rhode Island band to even come close to making it to the finals. In fact, some were even shocked that they invited us to participate in the first place.

It so happened that Margie's cousin, Moe Shore, was real tight in the Boston music scene. He had heard that some of the judges were impressed with our music. The first night, after we finished our forty-minute set, we came off the stage confident that we were the best band of that whole evening. Win or lose, we made a statement that we weren't some slouch band from Rhode Island. The applause and enthusiasm from the crowd showed us that if we could win the hearts of Boston fans, we could play to any crowd in the United States. Moe Shore came up to us right away and said, "You're going to win it all tonight! You were just too good not to." He also said, "Before this thing is over, you're going to the finals." Sure enough, at 1:00 a.m., WBCN disc jockeys announced the winner for the first round: Hi-Beams! I still get goose bumps today when I reflect upon that moment. We had gone up against some of the hottest up and coming bands, in one of the major music cities in the United States and walked out of there with a chance to move into the finals. We came back the next night; again we went up against some incredible bands and again we won. Now the newspapers in Rhode Island were starting to become believers. Even Phil Greene, who rarely left his studio, was in the crowd cheering us on, so proud of his production masterpiece, "Hyperactive."

A few nights later, round three of the competition was held. It included some real heavyweights in the industry. Some were former members of some big-time bands who were considered the Rumble "Favorites" on the card that night. The winners would go to the finals. After all the hype, all the emotion, and the multitude of bands that fell by the wayside along the way, this was OUR night. When we looked at the competition that we would be going up against, seasoned veterans on the Boston scene, one part of us thought that our chances of winning were slim to none, and the other side (which always seemed to surface at the right time) had an attitude of, "We're the hottest band out here and we're going to blow you away." Then about five minutes before we were to take the stage, we were in our dressing room alone. We looked at each other, and we put our arms around each other in a huddle. I said, "I don't know about you guys, but I say we're not going down tonight."

With that, my sister yelled out, "Let's kick their Boston Butts!"

We took the stage and played a real tight, high-energy set and hit them with our best songs back to back. When the night was over, there was only one band left standing: the "Hi Beams." We were going to play in the finals! The crowd of loyal fans that had followed us from Rhode Island practically blew-the-roof-off the place. They were completely awe-struck and extremely proud to be Rhode Islanders.

When our name was announced as the winner, we almost got trampled by our fans. We had reached a major milestone in our wild two years as a band. "You gotta sweat! You gotta grind!" Dad's philosophy, had paid off again, and I started to believe that we were unstoppable.

Think, for a moment, of some of the most difficult tasks that you have ever under-taken in your personal life and/or your greatest accomplishments realized to date. Perhaps it was a diet that resulted in a substantial amount of weight loss, or an exercise program that resulted in building muscle, burning fat and adding new untapped strength. Maybe it was a beautiful painting or sculpture that took months, if not years, to complete, or a hiking expedition or ambitious mountain climb that family and friends thought was a bit too ambitious. Maybe it was scraping all the paint off your two-story home and then painting it with two coats, or completing four painstaking years of college and then returning to complete your master's program. There are countless situations that involve commitment, persistence, focus and intensity.

For just a moment, reflect on those times in your life that involved a great commitment of your time and energy. These times in your life required discipline, focus and intensity that you never thought you possessed. Such accomplishments brought out a persistent nature in you that wouldn't take "no" for an answer. You just wouldn't quit! As a result you saw your task through to completion. Learning to be the best possible drummer that I could be, and competing on a professional level, was one of these times for me. It was ingrained in me as a child not to settle for second best! The grind mentality that my dad always spoke of had its foothold in my life.

With every difficult task and any great accomplishment that one personally realizes, there is a sequence of small beginnings, of tiny steps of progress along the way. Then, one day, you suddenly realize that you have accomplished something great. That's how our greatest, most ambitious dreams are accomplished and that's how you will accomplish your next great undertaking. It's always the small steps that lead you to large accomplishments and victory.

Climbing a mountain requires confidence, sure footedness, and balance. It's a climb of small, well-thought out steps and solid planning that doesn't necessarily take the fastest route to the top. The climb itself may seem illogical, unreasonable, dangerous, and downright crazy. But if the desire is there, who can stop you? Persistence and dedication are the tools needed for the difficult climb. Any great feat requires intense focus, the kind of focus and commitment levels that will allow you to shrug off the day-to-day problems that often cause us to get off track. You become so focused on what you're trying to accomplish that the little things just won't matter anymore. You slip and fall, you get back up. You break a critical piece of equipment, so you adjust, and work with what you have. Or, you realize you'll have to make some changes and alter the course you originally planned. BUT YOU DON'T STOP CLIMBING! This is the difference between those who finish and those who have stopped midstream. The successful are more committed to, and focused on, the dream. They believed they could succeed. I honestly can't imagine accomplishing anything of significance in my life if I weren't persistent and focused. When you commit to something, stay with it as long as you believe in that to which you committed. And, always go the extra mile. That persistent quality in you, whether learned or natural, will take you to new heights in your endeavors. I guarantee it!

During the course of writing this book, I started taking swimming lessons. It's just something that I always wanted to do. I taught myself to swim when I was a child by watching my older brothers and sister swim. I never took lessons from a professional. It's amazing, when you learn from a pro, just how much and how quickly you can learn if you put the time into it. It's equally amazing, how little I actually knew about the proper techniques of swimming. All these years, I swam incorrectly and I didn't realize just how enjoyable it could be, not to mention the cardiovascular and health benefits. My swimming instructor is forty-eight years old. She swims like a fish and teaches as if she's a staff sergeant in the Marines. During one of my lessons, I was literally gasping for air and I thought that my arms and legs were going to fall off. But, there she was, walking the length of the pool right beside me while yelling out her barrage of instructions, "Keep going! Get your air from explosive breaths in the water! Tuck in your pelvis! Full extension! Grab the water and pull! Keep going! Don't quit on me!"

Meanwhile, I was looking like an old walrus, desperately trying to reach land. I was saying to myself, "Quit on you, lady? Ha! I'm ready to quit on myself and take a nice sauna!" When I finished the lap, I looked up at her with a smile, while trying to catch my breath, and said "I was very content over the last forty-six years being a mediocre swimmer. Why am I doing this to myself?"

Her response was, "Because you always wanted it, but never took the time to do it. Now you're doing it and you can see the benefits and results."

As with any endeavor we take on, large or small, it's always the small steps, the small beginnings that bring us closer to the larger task at hand. Am I now in my instructor's league when it comes to swimming? Of course not! But I've made some major progress and I'm ready to step up to an advanced class. Who knows, maybe one year from now I may compete in the one-mile freestyle swim. I just might do that. I just might do that and go for the win!

Until you realize the commitment requirements and learn to focus, you might not see the dream through to completion. Until you become so persistent that you even surprise yourself and those closest to you, and you do it all with a level of intensity and passion that defies logic, you might just fall short and give up right before your time, right before you were going to complete the final lap. First, you have to dive into the pool head first! Then, you have to learn the right techniques that are much better than anything you thought you knew, and then you have to swim until you feel fatigue to the point that you want to quit and go home. But all who want to see their dream through to its completion have to come back to the pool the next day and jump in again. You'll be amazed at how much farther you'll go and how much faster and sleeker with less of a struggle you'll glide through the water. Just remember one thing. When you start making those incredible strides, you have to come up for air. You have to realize that "Rome wasn't built in a day." Neither are dreams. Small beginnings are a great place to start.

That is how it was with the Hi Beams. We had a dream. We focused on the goals we set. We let nothing stand in our way. Our perseverance and perspiration paid off. We were a new sensation, off to stardom!

Hi Beams, first promo shot, 1980
L-R: Me, Margie, Lou, and Deb

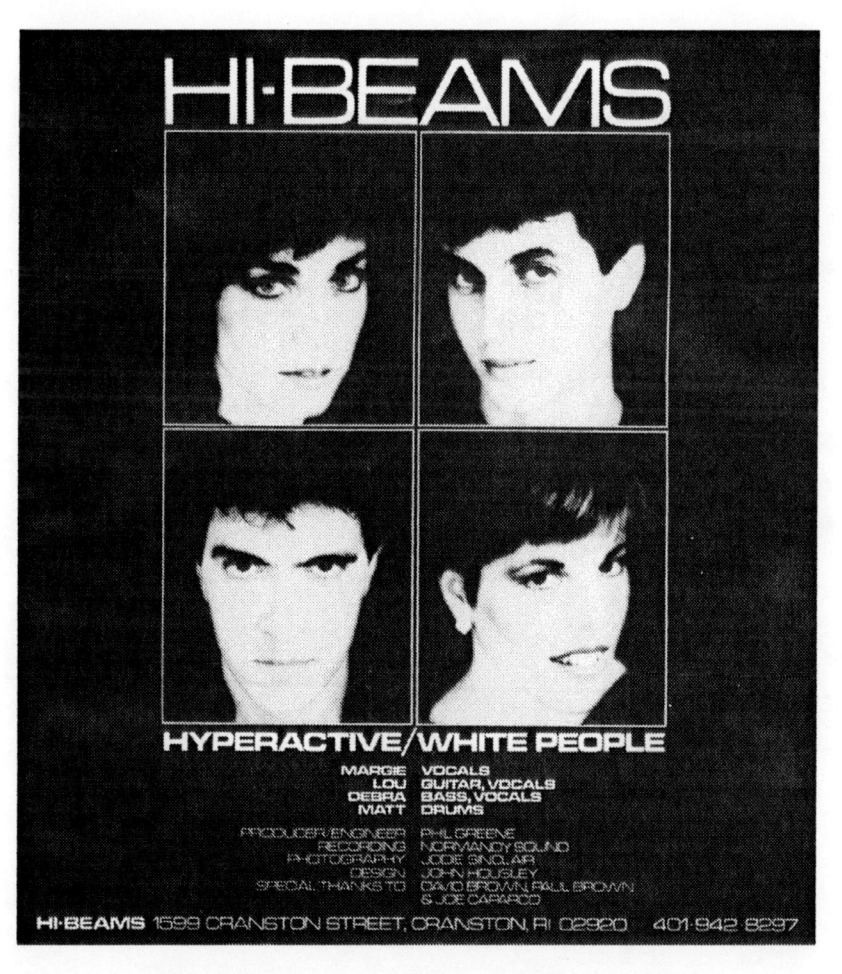

Hi Beams, first smash single "Hyperactive," 1981

Me on drums, Margie in leopard at the RAT in Boston

Chapter Ten

Tina Turner, Margie, and Jesus

"Only be strong, and very courageous, then you will make your way prosperous, and then you will have good success."
Joshua 1:7-8

The finals of the WBCN Rumble came down to just two bands: The Hi Beams and Limbo Race {What a stupid name}. To no one's surprise, the final night at the very popular, the very vogue, Club Spit was packed to capacity. By this time we had been featured in all the major newspapers in Rhode Island and Boston and had a huge contingency of loyal fans and family who came out to see us make history.

We went out and played an incredible set. The crowd went bonkers from the second we hit the stage and never stopped until we left the stage. Next, Limbo Race played a decent set. They really and truly were nothing special. Quite frankly, it was a mystery to me how they made it this far. Never-the-less, it was their night! Our long ride on the WBCN Rumble train had come to an end as Limbo Race won and we were awarded first runner-up.

While we were disappointed, it didn't last more than a day. Once everything settled in our minds and we read all the reviews over the next few days, we realized our accomplishments were enormous. Being first runner-up turned out to be a blessing in disguise. We were awarded recording time at the prestigious Boston recording studio, Syncro-Sound, owned by Rick Ocasek, lead singer and songwriter for the national recording artists and Boston's own, The Cars. We booked our time in Syncro-Sound immediately, and decided that we would use the free recording time wisely to release another single. We finished in a little over two weeks. We had another hit on our hands, a new hot single called, "Live in Shadows." It was, without a doubt, our best studio work to date. To make us even more marketable we immediately started to work on a video to accompany our new hit song. With a decent low budget video in hand, a very strong sound track, accompanied by our success in the WBCN Rumble, and still riding the wave of success from "Hyperactive," we had more agents/managers and club owners approaching us than we could ever have imagined. Within two months, "Live in Shadows" became the #1 most requested song on WBCN's local showcase of bands, which featured bands from all over New England. We also started to play every top club in the Boston scene as a headliner.

With everything moving three-hundred miles an hour, I didn't have much time to think about fruit and produce. Many of the same drummers that I had once envied became quite intrigued with my unorthodox style that seemed to drive a song like a locomotive. I had made my mark as a legitimate professional drummer and I was feeling pretty good about it. We had achieved everything that we set out to accomplish in Rhode Island and Boston. We were receiving rave reviews from music critics. We had weekly interviews on radio stations, along with regular rotation air play of our singles, "Hyperactive" and "Live in Shadows."

Our club dates were booked solid, and we could demand more money from the larger, more prestigious clubs. Our video was being shown in sixteen states on local music networks. It was now time to hit the New York music scene, where we felt that we could be seen by all the top record labels. We were already receiving phone calls and getting some strong interest from the smaller Boston labels. But, we had our sights set on the bigger labels that could catapult us into stardom.

In April of 1983, we received a phone call from our friend, fan, and part-time promoter, Dan Savage. Dan came from a very wealthy New York family. He had recently graduated from Brown University. He was smart, articulate, and savvy, and he was really into our band. He wanted to become our full-time agent and promoter. But, we weren't sure that he had enough experience to take us to the next level and land us a record deal. He quickly proved us wrong when out of the blue came his phone call that blew our minds! "Hey, guys," he said "how would you like to be the opening act for Tina Turner's comeback tour this summer?"

At first we thought that he was joking or smoking! But, he came right back and said, "Guys, I'm dead serious. Her management heard your music and they want you."

We told him that we would think about it. There was dead silence on the other end of the phone, and with that we all started laughing and my brother-in-law, Lou, quickly said to him, "We're kidding, Dan! Where and when? We'll be there!" We then looked at each other and began to jump around like little kids on a free shopping spree in a toy store. The local newspapers soon got hold of the story and it just added to the hysteria and buzz levels that were going around about our band.

Tina Turner's comeback tour was scheduled to begin at the elite club, "The Ritz" in New York City, which held approximately 3,000 people and was riding the wave of being the top nightclub in the city, maybe the country. We had approximately forty-five days to start preparing musically and to line up record company A&R (Artist and Repertoire) people to check us out. We also worked extremely hard on our stage presence and music, spending long nights in our studio practicing. The big night finally came and it was everything, and more, than we expected. Anyone who was anyone in the rock'n'roll world was there on opening night. The entire second floor of the club was blocked off specifically for Tina's special guests and ...well...us, of course, since we were her opening act. So standing next to me in the course of the night was Keith Richards from the Rolling Stones; David Bowie, dressed in a white suit, cheering on Tina with all-out enthusiasm; Richie Havens, who was actually a nice guy and very complimentary to us, and several other rock and movie stars, all there to support Tina.

We rocked the place and were quite a contrast to Tina's show. She was singing and dancing to a more choreographed Las Vegas-type act. We had a definite rock, new wave, mild punk rock, look and sound, only with more of a pop song feel. Margie and Deb rocked on with their unique style and great stage presence, while Lou and I just did what we did best: play hard, fast and loud rock and roll. Not only could Margie sing like there was no tomorrow, but she could move on stage as well as any female rock singer in the country. Tina, on the other hand, was dressed in a gold glitter short dress to show off those million-dollar legs and her gold and green glitter back-up singers, who resembled mermaids hyped up on caffeine, ran around the stage like headless chickens trying to keep up with an ageless and fit Tina as they rolled their arms and kicked their legs to a sped-up version of "Rolling On The River." Observing the contrast of the two bands, someone along the way must have noticed that we were hip and Tina's style was old hat! It was quite obvious that "rock and roll" and "Las Vegas Show Girl" types don't mesh. People wanted to see Tina rock the way they knew she could. Her "What's Love Got to Do with It" Tour became just that, Tina Turner belting out rock and roll with black leather, wild hair, no Las Vegas leg kicks, and no glittering mermaids in the background running around the stage, just pure "rock'n'roll." She was incredible and the rest is history!

It was somewhere between the Tina Turner comeback tour, opening for Belinda Carlyle and the Go, Go's, opening for Iggy Pop, and receiving numerous phone calls from A&M Records (co-owned by Herb Albert) and CBS Records asking us for more and more material, that Margie started to change. I was too strung out to really notice the seriousness of it, but she started going to church. Now for a Jewish girl to go to church and not synagogue was strange enough in itself. She was also reading her Bible every spare minute that she could find. During this time period, she repeatedly told me that she wasn't happy with the direction we were going. She didn't like singing some of the lyrics of our songs. She wasn't happy with herself. Margie was sick of playing to unruly crowds at one o'clock in the morning, who, the drunker they got, the better we sounded. She also started to seek some real-life answers to questions such as, "Why am I here? What is the real purpose of my life? Isn't there more for me than just seeking a record deal and singing rock and roll?" Margie found out the answers to all those questions and dedicated her life to the Lord. Her conversion to Christianity back then, was as real as it is today. Through it all, she was just as determined for us to stay in love and not let anything come between us as we continued on our wild, roller-coaster ride with the Hi-Beams.

Then it happened! One summer afternoon, when I walked through the door of our apartment, after coming back from drum practice at the studio, she suddenly hit me right between the eyes, like a ton of bricks, with this statement. "I know that you think I've became some religious fanatic. But, the truth is, I can't do this anymore. For the rest of my life I only want to use my voice and my talents to glorify God! I'm quitting the band!"

Now, had she said this to me just two years earlier, maybe even one year earlier, I may have been ecstatic at the thought of working with bananas and peaches again, but instead I yelled out, "NOW???... Now??? After all this work! After all this time! After subjecting my body to the two hour concerts and staying up until five o'clock in the morning, playing every dive within a two-hundred mile radius! After the success of "Hyperactive," "Live In Shadows," and Tina Turner and all the airplay and rave reviews? NOW? You want to quit? After we are so close to signing a record deal, after all the success and accomplishments and realizing your dream, YOU WANT TO QUIT? YOU DON'T QUIT NOW; IT MAKES NO SENSE."

Margie looked at me and just quietly said, "I'm sorry, I just can't do this anymore."

I decided that I would stay on with the band and we would look for another lead singer. Margie agreed to play out the next three months of gigs that we had booked and were obligated to play.

The following few weeks were very stressful especially when the same *Providence Journal* writer who was touting us as the next signed band to a major label wrote, "Hi-Beams, a band on the verge, coming off a very strong single, opening for Tina Turner's Comeback Tour and achieving what most bands only envy, are disbanding, or at least regrouping, as band member and lead singer Margie Olerio quits due to her Born Again Christian lifestyle." After receiving seventy-five phone calls throughout the morning and afternoon, from family members asking me if my wife was okay and was I in need of any help, I knew that my life was changing dramatically, right before my eyes.

I knew that everyone was thinking that my wife had gone off the deep end and had become a Jesus freak. I went upstairs into our apartment and I systematically tore up every religious tract and magazine that was out in the open. Then I found the Bible. I looked at it and hid it under a stack of books in our spare room. When Margie came home, walked in the door and saw the torn literature all over the floor, she welled up with tears, but didn't say a word.

I needed to talk to someone, so I left our apartment. I took a walk and made a brief stop at my aunt Ellie's house. She lived just a few blocks away. She too had read the newspaper article and had her own thoughts on the subject. She boldly said to me, "Matthew, don't throw away the best thing that ever happened to you in your life! Your wife is something special."

Once again, family played an important part in my life. I only lasted about two more weeks as a member of the Hi-Beams. I told my sister and brother-in-law that it was all over for me too. I just couldn't do it without Margie.

Without my wife by my side, nothing else mattered to me. There was no dream, no gig, no single, no rock star status worth coming between me and the flowered-dress hippie girl I had married seven years earlier. She stuck by my side when we first met and I only had fifty cents in my pocket and a '62 green Ford truck. She stood right by me and worked side by side as we sold fruits and vegetables on Park Avenue to the frenzied crowds. She was the girl of my dreams and I wasn't about to abandon her when she needed me most. Besides, I was madly in love with her (and still am) and knew deep down inside that this was the right decision for the both of us. We left the life of rock and roll and we never looked back.

Just like that, it was over. I was twenty-seven years old and had already realized two individuals' dreams, my dad's fruit and produce dream and Margie's dream to be a famous singer. I was frail and sickly looking, flat broke, with no career. I was no longer a rock star and was still going through the shock of my wife's major religious transformation.

My brother Al, by this time, had built quite a name for himself and ran an extremely successful Italian restaurant business on Park Avenue called Olerio's. He immediately offered me a job to wait tables. From opening for Tina Turner only a few months earlier and signing autographs for loyal fans and groupies, I now found myself back on Park Avenue. Only this time, I wasn't the reigning "King of Produce," who took on the world. I wasn't the rock star who would occasionally go in for dinner at my brother's restaurant when we weren't traveling. Instead I was a waiter dressed in black polyester pants, a white tuxedo shirt and bow tie. I felt that I had sunk to an all-time low in my life. I thought it was all a bad dream and I'd be waking up any minute.

MELLOW PEACHES, THREE POUNDS FOR A DOLLAR

My first night on the job at my brother's restaurant, just before opening time, I stood alone in the dining room and stared out the window at my reflection. I vividly remember whispering under my breath, "You have to pick yourself up, Matt, and do something! You can't quit now! You can't quit now!"

The restaurant doors soon opened and my new career started as a waiter. "Good evening, welcome to Olerio's. My name is Matt! I'll be your server this evening. Let me tell you about tonight's specials."

Hi Beams hanging out backstage at The Ritz in New York during the Tina Turner comeback tour

16,425 Days Remaining

    I thought it might be beneficial to briefly speak to those of you who may have recently lost your job, as a result of the epidemic called, "corporate downsizing," or perhaps who may be going through a midlife "I hate my job and I want out," crisis. Losing your career, especially after you felt you were a loyal and dedicated employee, can be very disheartening. It can also cause a tremendous amount of resentment, stress, and bitterness. Many of my close friends have been affected by this process. I can see a familiar pattern in all of them. Anxiety leads to brief bouts of depression, uncertainty, feelings of inadequacy as a breadwinner of the family, low self-esteem, and so on. I can tell you it's not a healthy place to be, and it needs to be left behind, once and for all.

    One may ask, "How does one escape from the grips of this too familiar plague to society?" The first thing you need to realize is that you are not alone. The second thing is to know there is a light at the end of the tunnel, and to get there you have to start moving towards it right here and now. If a company/employer or business partner did wrong by you, then welcome to the club. The more you dwell on it, the more you're expanding the wrong that was done to you initially, until those feelings become like weeds in a garden that eventually grow vast enough to choke the healthy plants. If you're allowing these thoughts to consume your mind and your precious time, then it's just as though you're still working for "Them," <u>only now you're not getting paid.</u> Let it go! Move forward and take action! Remove the ball and chain that's around your crushed ego. We're here to take on the world. Your job loss, or your dissatisfaction with your career, can be your turning point in the business of transforming your life. You have a choice here. Will you keep it as a stumbling block, a festering sore, or step over it, and make it a stepping stone, a building block in your life? By letting go, what you're really saying to yourself is, "Ok, I'm done fighting it. I'm through mourning and drowning in self pity. It's over, and I finally need to move on with my life." Once you say that and mean it, then climb on board the truck of life, because we're ready to start moving out some massive loads of peaches.

    I want you to guesstimate how many more years you feel you may have left on this earth. Sounds crazy, right? Not really, it's a fact of life that we eventually complete our term on this earth. Once you look at your life in that realm, you'll want to accomplish much more with the time you have remaining. After you guesstimate your time remaining (in years), I want you to multiply that number by 365. For example, if you're hoping for forty more years, then you are looking at about 16,425 days remaining. That's 16,425 days to get it together. Now that's a whole lot of days...or is it? The point I'm making is crystal clear. Procrastination leads to stagnation! That will lead you to one day, waking up and saying to yourself, "Where did all the years go?" If you're waiting for that, "lucky break," just remember that luck comes, <u>when preparation meets opportunity!</u>

Take your number of days and make a big, bold poster of it. Date it with today's date, and hang it in your bathroom right next to your think tank. You'll notice after a week or so that your number isn't going up. One could say that the point of this exercise is rather basic; <u>make the most of every hour of every day.</u> But my point goes much deeper than that. Our lives on this earth are passing, with each hour, and we have choices to make on how we spend our precious time. You need to recognize more than ever that your time is extremely valuable. In fact, <u>it's priceless.</u> If you want to see real change come about, and see your dreams unfold before your eyes, then start keeping close tabs on how and where you are spending your time. To maximize your productivity takes wisdom and time, and the only one you can buy that time from is YOU. For example, waking up an hour earlier, taking fifteen minutes less time for lunch, working an hour later than you have in the past. That scenario alone just gave you two hours and fifteen minutes more per day. Multiplied by five days equals 11 hours and fifteen minutes more per week, and multiplied by fifty-two weeks allows you 585 hours more per year, or twenty-four extra days annually to be more productive and focused on dream building.

16,425

Chapter Eleven

Stocks, Bonds, Houses and Flowers... Again?

"Life can only be understood backwards but it must be lived forward."

Soren Kierkegaard

Waiting on tables was a humbling experience for me. But, through that experience, I still learned. I felt like my world was turned upside down. All I could do was focus 24/7 on how I was going to rebuild my life better than I ever had. At twenty-seven years of age I had tasted success and lived through the agony of defeat. Looking back, on that first day of work at my brother's restaurant, staring out of the window and seeing my reflection, talking to myself, I know now, that it was a definite turning point in my life. I knew then and there that I wasn't going to give up! I knew more than ever before, that I was going to challenge myself to the max!

One morning after looking at my worn-out body in the mirror, I said to myself, "You look more like sixty-seven years old, rather than twenty-seven."

I joined the YMCA the next day and started weight training. For me it was simple, I just found the biggest, strongest guys in the gym, and asked a lot of questions. We became friends. I started to work out with them. Because I worked nights at the restaurant I had my mornings free so I took full advantage of it. I started to become obsessed with weight training. I had left the band pale and frail, weighing just 160 pounds on my 6'3" frame. Within six months of intense weight training I bulked up to 190 pounds. Within a year I was a muscular 210 pounds. I had put the same effort into weight training that I had into drumming. Now I felt healthy and strong.

During this time period one of my older brothers, Louis, asked me if I had ever thought of looking into a career as a stock and bond broker. He had a close friend in the business up in New Hampshire working with E.F. Hutton who was doing quite well. I told him that I'd certainly be interested in looking into it. With that, my brother arranged a meeting for me to visit his friend in Portsmouth. I immediately became fascinated with the business and the thought of being a stock broker ignited a new spark in me. There were just a few obstacles in the way, a few BIG obstacles. I was a college dropout and I knew absolutely nothing about the stock and bond business. Then again, that had never stopped me before... I set a goal to be hired by one of the top five major Wall Street brokerage firms within six months of that initial meeting in New Hampshire.

With whatever extra money that I could make from waiting tables, I started buying some pretty decent suits. I had a pretty good eye for fashion and my newly transformed body allowed me to get into a more athletic cut suit. I also started to study on my own, everything that I could get my hands on pertaining to Wall Street, stocks, bonds, mutual funds, municipal and corporate bonds. To me, it was learning a whole new language, but I was more determined than ever.

During this time I also started to change spiritually. Unlike Margie, I was raised Roman Catholic. I had always believed in Jesus and my mother had always taught me the power of prayer. But Margie's transformation was different. While I was actually aware of the comments made behind her back, "religious fanatic" or "Jesus freak," no one knew better than I, what was going on. My marriage was better than ever. These were becoming the happiest days of my life. The more soul searching and questioning that I did on my own, the more I realized that God also had a plan for me. In addition, I realized that having a personal relationship with my Heavenly Father was the greatest thing that I had ever experienced in my life. If someone wanted to laugh at me behind my back, then so be it. I wasn't as bold as Margie about proclaiming my newfound relationship with Jesus, but nonetheless, I knew that it was real. I knew God was answering prayer in our lives.

Dressed like a high-profile executive and with a newfound confidence, I set out to apply to every major brokerage firm in Rhode Island. My first stop was Shearson Lehman Brothers. From there, I interviewed at Dean Witter, then at Merrill Lynch, Morgan Stanley,

Paine Webber, Tucker Anthony and Smith Barney. After months of interviews, going back two and three times, taking four-hour aptitude tests, the results were all the same. No college diploma, no background in economics, no can do. My background as a fruit and produce man/rock & roll drummer, now working as a waiter, just wasn't cutting the mustard. Many in my own family started to think I was chasing a rainbow and living in fantasy land by thinking that I could ever land such a job. Even if I did, I was told that without a formal education, I would never pass the complex Series Seven exam required in order to be registered with the NASD.

Discouraged, but still determined, I booked a flight and interviewed at several brokerage houses in Ft. Lauderdale, Florida, not far from where my parents had settled in and retired in Boca Raton. Margie and I were both willing to move. She had family of her own in that area. But after two months of return interviews, the results were the same as in Rhode Island. I made one more attempt in New Hampshire, but to no avail.

I decided that I would try one more round in Rhode Island. My persistence paid off. I went back to the first brokerage house I had interviewed with, Shearson Lehman Brothers. It just so happened that the manager that had interviewed me, had recently transferred to New York, so the regional vice president of New England and New York just happened to be in the office. He took an immediate liking to me after I laid it all out on the line and told him my background and my frustration in not being able to break in to the industry. The last thing I said to him, before I left the office, as I looked him in the eyes and gave him a firm handshake was, "I'm a fast learner and a hard worker! I won't let you down if you give me the opportunity."

He called me the next morning at home and said, "You're hired, report to the World Trade Center office for a briefing in two weeks."

I said, "Thank you, sir."

His last words before he hung up the phone were said with a genuine heartfelt laugh, "Any guy who can sell fruit and produce the way you did and then open for Tina Turner deserves a shot, in my book."

I wanted to pick Margie up and spin her around our kitchen. But, there was other good news she had told me just the day before…she was pregnant. I was walking on cloud nine! I had just been hired by

MELLOW PEACHES, THREE POUNDS FOR A DOLLAR

Shearson Lehman Brothers, one of the most prestigious firms on Wall Street, and I was going to be a father. I had reached my goal of landing a job in the six-month time frame that I had set. I was healthy as an ox and I was once again ready to take on the world.

My next challenge was to pass the Series Seven Exam. Without passing it, I would no longer have a job. That was it, plain and simple. Pass it, and I would go on to train for seven straight weeks at the World Trade Center and walk the floor of the New York Stock Exchange. Fail it, and I'd be back to wearing my bow tie and polyester pants as a waiter.

With the same sense of trepidation that I felt when I thought that I wasn't good enough at drumming, I now set about to pass this eight-hour Series Seven Exam. Shearson Lehman provided me with a study kit, complete with thirty booklets. They contained every piece of material that could possibly be on the exam, along with sample tests to take after completing each booklet. I remember opening up the kit and staring at each book intensely: *Municipal Bonds, Options, NASD Rules and Regulations, Corporate Bonds, Stocks, Margin Requirements, Limited Partnerships, Open End Mutual Funds, Closed End Mutual Funds, Treasuries,* and *Annuities*. Book after book, page after page, it was a whole new language. I had three months to study before the test. I was beginning to think, "How am I ever going to absorb and retain all this information?"

At the initial briefing in New York, I saw hundreds of newly hired individuals that came in from all over the country. We filled the conference room at corporate headquarters at the World Trade Center. It didn't take me long to realize that I was the only one without a college education. Most of them came from very solid financial backgrounds. Some of them had just completed their master's degree or were professionals, such as lawyers and bankers looking for a challenging career change.

I was instructed that I had to report to the Shearson Lehman office in Providence once a week to let the manager know how I was progessing with my studies. The rest of the time I could devote to preparing for the exam wherever I felt the most comfortable. I chose the library. I also called upon a man that I knew was an excellent teacher in any subject, and whom I thought would be willing to tutor me. It was Uncle Eddie. Yes, Uncle Eddie, Margie's Uncle who ran the downtown supermarket and gave me the pre-World War II tables for my open air market. Once again, the words of my dad rang out loud and clear in my mind. "You want anything in this life, you gotta grind, you gotta work twelve hour days." To me, even twelve hour days just wouldn't give me enough time. Being faced with fatherhood and the fear of losing a job that I had worked so hard to land, set me on a fierce pace. I was studying from 5:00 AM until midnight. I only took breaks to eat, to go to the bathroom, and to do pushups. I realized that I was being challenged mentally, more than I ever had been in my entire life.

On the day of the big test, I was ready. I had driven to Boston the night before and stayed in a hotel right up the street from where the test was given. I woke up early, said my prayers, and was one of the first ones to enter the building.

My manager called me three days later and said, "Welcome aboard, son! Congratulations, you passed the Series Seven."

The feeling of accomplishment, at that point in my life, was overwhelming. I was in my apartment. I hung up the phone and looked over at my beautiful, pregnant Margie, and gave her a long hug as tears of joy came down her cheeks. We both realized more than ever, right there and then in our kitchen, the awesome faithfulness of God. I was to take a flight out one week later to start a seven-week training session in New York. I had to report in on the Monday after Easter Sunday. Although I was on the Shearson Lehman payroll, I was just paid a base salary paid during my study and training period. There still wasn't quite enough money to get me through the seven weeks' training plus provide Margie with enough money to live on. Knowing it was Easter week, I came up with a plan. Just up the street from my former outdoor open air fruit market on Park Avenue was a vacant lot. I put the whole deal together in three days, one huge trailer, a big "A" frame sign, seven long tables, and a peddling license to sell flowers. I then went to three different growers, negotiated almost as well as my dad, and purchased seven hundred tulips, five hundred mums, three hundred hyacinths and four hundred Easter lilies. My sign went up just like the old days, when I was a teenager: Tulips $2.99. By 2:00 p.m. Easter Sunday I had sold every last flower. I pocketed a little over two thousand dollars profit. I gave half of it to Margie, then I took a 4:00 p.m. flight out to New

York.

I came home seven weeks later with a new found knowledge of the business. I felt as though I had worked harder than anyone else in my class. Within six months, I was second in the nation as a rookie in opening up new accounts and having money under management. Within two years I was offered jobs by three different brokerage houses, the same firms that had previously turned me down. Each one made me very attractive offers and competed against each other with sizable signing bonuses. While I felt loyalty to Shearson Lehman Brothers, I just could not justify not taking one of the offers complete with a private office in the newest high rise building in Providence. I signed on with Prudential Bache Securities and was making a six-figure income before my thirtieth birthday.

The truth of the matter was, I absolutely hated the corporate structure. The meetings were boring. You relied on analysts who were seldom right. We went through managers every six months who would come in with bells on trying to persuade me to sell packaged products such as limited partnerships, about which they that they knew nothing. It was a game where the most important thing to the firm was, "What did you sell for me today and how much revenue and commissions did you generate? I felt the sincerity behind most managers was suspect because many who came to Providence saw it only as a stepping stone to a much larger, profitable office in Boston, Hartford, or other major cities. Having said that, there were also a handful of some very dedicated, stand-up managers who worked hard and made Providence their permanent homes.

After the savings and loan crisis, and the crash of 1987, I lost a great deal of money for myself, my family, and friends. I came to the realization that, I am who I am. I'm an entrepreneur and I have to call my own shots, good, bad or indifferent. I decided that I would never rely on someone else's opinion to decide my fate. I resigned in 1989. While I felt terrible about investments that I had made for myself and family members that went sour, I had also made some very good investments for the hundreds of clients that I was leaving behind. I also took with me a wealth of knowledge that became vital and helpful as I started on a new adventure in my life. Everyone around me now thought that I was the one who had gone off the deep end. But, I had a plan and there was no way I was turning back.

During my time at Shearson Lehman I became very interested in real estate. I started dabbling here and there buying and selling land. I also started to build several homes on speculation, and the business intrigued me. After moving over to Prudential Bache, the pace became too overwhelming. So, I put my real estate business, called North American Homes Inc., on hold. However, homebuilding had the same effect on me as fruits, vegetables and flowers. I could not get it out of my mind, no matter how hard I tried. I loved the smell of fresh lumber. I loved seeing a piece of land transformed, step by step, as the building process evolved the land from a vacant lot, into a beautiful home with a yard complete with swing set and family. There was such a feeling of accomplishment and reward. I learned, that as a general contractor, I could create something from nothing. I also learned the value of surrounding myself with the most reliable and finest craftsman in the trade, even if it meant paying more money up front per subcontractor. In the long run, I saved money. I also loved making the sale, putting out my own signs in front of the properties. It reminded me of Park Avenue, only these were "Mellow Houses, Three Hundred Tons for $250,000."

The day I resigned from Prudential Bache Securities, I was stepping out in faith, and I was determined that I would never work for anyone again for the rest of my life, no matter what it would take.

The love of my life — Margie

Rejection: Friend or Foe?

We have already discussed how set backs and disappointments can often be debilitating and stop you dead in your tracks. Now let's discuss dealing with rejection. Rejection can have the same negative effect if you don't learn to use it to your advantage. In sales, the greatest salesmen in the world learn quickly that every "no" that they receive from a prospective buyer brings them closer to a "yes." So, for example, if you happen to be a mortgage broker cold calling, offering home equity loans, and in the course of a day you've already been turned down [rejected] eighty-seven times, I can guarantee that you're getting closer to making a sale. It's the law of averages theory and it works. At the same time, if the interest rate you're touting is a percentage point higher than the industry average, you could be in for a very long day. Believing in yourself or in the product you are touting is one thing, not seeing the forest for the trees, is another story. In other words, know your obstacles and know how to overcome them, so your chances of winning are greater than your competitor's. Use rejection as a spring board to keep surging ahead and for improving yourself or your product. If it becomes obvious that change is needed, then make those necessary adjustments quickly and move on. Rejection stops many a dreamer from reaching his goals. Rejection, if not harnessed correctly, leads to disappointment, which leads to a downward spiral in your productivity. Rejection, disappointment, and failure are distant cousins. Constantly dwelling on them only exacerbates the situation and has absolutely no benefit to turning your current situation and life around. Forge ahead with courage and a clear mind. Let rejection be your friend, not your adversary.

Chapter Twelve

"Shayna, Gospel Music and Baseball"

"Trust in the Lord and do good; dwell in the land, and feed on His faithfulness. Delight yourself also in the Lord, and He will give you the desires of your heart."
                                                     Psalm 37: 3-4

During the summer of 1993, Margie became pregnant with our third child. By this time our oldest son, Matthew, was eight years old and James was six. It had been quite some time since we heard babies crying or changed diapers! We were as excited as young kids and prayed that we would be blessed with a precious little girl. A few months before Margie knew she was pregnant; she closed her eyes to go to sleep. She immediately sat up in bed and said with a big smile, "I just saw the name, "Shayna," written in script. That's going to be our daughter's name." (Shayna means beautiful in Hebrew.) Now, she was convinced more than ever that she was carrying a girl and Shayna would be her name. North American Homes was going stronger than ever. While I was running the family business, Margie was busy raising two sons and getting the spare bedroom ready for the arrival of our baby, Shayna.

It was Feb. 16, 1994, when Margie went into labor. I drove her to the hospital. Within a few hours the doctor held up our newborn child, smiled and said, "It's a girl!" We were both overjoyed and ecstatic. But, the joy lasted only for a few minutes. We both watched nervously while a team of doctors hovered around our little girl on a nearby table. We immediately knew something was wrong. More doctors entered the room. Then one of the female physicians turned and walked over to us with Shayna in her arms. She gently handed her to Margie and said in a whispering, calming voice, "Your little girl has Down syndrome." My legs buckled and I immediately thought, "No, no way could this be happening to us." I was in a state of disbelief! Having a Down syndrome child was always one of my biggest fears. I grew up with a Down's child in my neighborhood and always considered that having one was a burden too great to bear. Within just a few hours, the halls in the hospital maternity ward were filled with our Jewish and Italian families, friends and our pastor. Family had always come through for us. But, where was God in all of this? I felt abandoned! I questioned my own faith.

I went home from the hospital that evening alone. Our two sons were staying at my brother's home and Margie was in the hospital recovering from C-section surgery. I lay on my bed and just stared at the ceiling and thought, "How could everything be going so well in our lives and then have this happen to us?" I was devastated and basking in self- pity. I lay there and stared into nothingness. I questioned the same God who had proved Himself faithful time and time again. I don't remember falling asleep. But, I'll never forget waking up! I abruptly sat up in my bed and as if I had been given an intense attitude adjustment from God Almighty while I was sleeping. I had a sudden urge to get back to the hospital and hold my daughter in my arms. I suddenly realized, with a strong, clear awareness, that my daughter was not a curse, but, in fact, was a blessing and a special gift to our family. I went from mourning and anguish to a feeling of peace and contentment. There was no denying what I had experienced. It was as if I had been given a new set of eyes and a new mind-set as I realized that my life wasn't over. I spoke out loud to myself, "I have it all, and who am I to feel pity for myself? Shayna's a special gift from God just like my two boys are. I'm going to the hospital and give my little baby all the love she deserves from me."

I just made one stop on the way there. It was to the local drug store to purchase two boxes of, "It's a Girl" Cigars. For the next few days, everyone I came in contact with didn't really know what to say to me. Their approach was more like we were mourning a death in the family, rather than celebrating a birth. I knew it was awkward for them. I understood, so I just smiled and said, "Have a cigar! She's beautiful!"

Statements of faith, about miracles of divine intervention, and being touched by God, are often quickly explained away as, "coincidence," or perceived by many as, "a naïve way of thinking." But to me, I could never deny the reality of how God touched me, and spoke to my heart, regarding Shayna's birth. It's my own testimony. Nobody can take it away or explain it away. Margie came home from the hospital with our little angel. Our home was literally filled with fruit baskets and flowers. For the next few weeks, family and friends filled our home too, willing to lend a helping hand.

When Shayna was one month old, my entire family came to our home. Counting all the grandchildren, there were thirty-one of us. At dinner time my dad stood up at the head of the table and asked if we could all stand up, hold hands, and say grace together. Never before had my father led us in prayer. With his voice quivering, my dad thanked God for our precious little Shayna. I had experienced the second miracle in thirty days as I watched our entire family reunited, holding hands, and praying together. The rough, tough dad, that I had known all my life, was melted by our little baby girl and was absolutely head over heels in love with her.

Shayna was a miracle, just like our two boys. She brought our family together closer than ever. She gave me a whole new outlook on my life. Though she was healthy, for the most part, at age two and a half, she ran into some major complications with her digestive system. As a result, she went through two major surgeries and stayed in Hasbro Children's Hospital for thirty-two days. With her weight down to just fourteen pounds, she ended up in intensive care and was hanging on to her precious little life by a thread. It was at that time that I saw the power of prayer in a way that I had never before experienced it. A Chinese Christian gentleman, who barely spoke English, called our home. We knew of him from our son's school. We knew of his deep faith which was evident from the persecution that he had experienced for his beliefs when he lived in mainland China. He spoke to me in his best English possible, "Mr. Matt, have no fear! Tonight, there will be eight thousand Chinese Christians praying for your daughter, Shayna, over the Internet. God will answer and she will live to be healthy and strong."

As I'm writing this book Shayna, is nine years old. She's in the second grade, weighs a healthy sixty pounds, and is incredibly strong. She's a raving beauty and we marvel every day at her accomplishments. She has taught me the real meaning of courage, determination, and unconditional love. She has inspired our family members to reach for our greatest dreams, and to know that all things are possible.

After Shayna was born, I began to see things a bit differently in my life, especially in my career. I also came to the sudden realization that my children were growing older and I felt a sense of urgency to start spending more time with them and less time on the job sites, working painstaking hours with customers, developing their plans for custom homes. I was determined that my grown children would never say, "My dad never spent any time with me."

As much as my business meant to me, my family and marriage towered over it. Besides all that, Margie needed me around a lot more as Shayna got older. A special needs child requires care that I cannot explain in one paragraph. There is always a steady flow of physical therapists, speech therapists, occupational therapists, and state aid representatives coming to our home. We always seem to be fighting and lobbying for more care for our child. Nevertheless, I wouldn't trade my life (raising our family) with anyone in the world. I truly consider it a privilege.

I stopped working seven days a week. I placed my "open houses" in the hands of real estate agents. I also hired a site manager to look after the day-to-day operations of the business. Now he was ordering materials, coordinating sub contractors, managing cost control, and keeping the job sites clean and organized. It took a big load off of my shoulders and allowed me to focus more on the selling and financing ends of the business. I also had more time to scope out land deals. With my extra time in the evenings, I started coaching my two sons in Little League Baseball. I also discovered a newfound love, in songwriting. I even bought a new set of drums and a piano to help me along. While I still worked long days, I was trying to work smarter and was finding more and more time to spend with Margie and our children.

By 1996 I had written an entire album of songs. Margie and I went back into the recording studio with none other than the legendary Phil Greene. Only this time, he was an older, mellower chap, and he really dug our new music. Fifteen years had gone by since we had worked with him as members of the Hi Beams, recording, "Hyperactive." I wrote an upbeat gospel album that could appeal to all age groups, but aimed at an older crowd. The album, entitled, "I Waited for the Lord," took a little over one year to complete. Margie's sister, Tamara, and her husband, Jim, designed the front cover and I spent countless hours laying out all the lyrics and liner notes. I took the final mix (recording) to New York City to have it mastered. We hired an independent manufacturer to print the cover, insert the sleeve, label and press the actual CD. We released it with no great expectations, in the spring of 1997. Margie, who for years had given benefit concerts and shared her testimony, was also realizing those days were quickly coming to an end. As Shayna grew older and required more and more of our time, we decided we wouldn't do concerts for awhile. Several Christian radio stations around the country began playing our new album, but our time was so consumed with family obligations, that we had little interest in following up the airplay with concert appearances.

In the meantime, our sons began to take baseball seriously and I really enjoyed coaching their teams. Margie would often suggest, that I was living out my dream to be a professional baseball player through my two boys, in the same way my dad lived out his fruit and produce dream through me. I would always respond, "It's their dream, not mine." I coached with the same level of intensity that I did everything else. Some probably thought that I was an overzealous, obnoxious, loud Italian. After the games (which we usually won) I would often get the cold shoulder or hear comments such as, "You take this too seriously, they're just kids." Truth was, I really had a great rapport with the kids. I was strict and I demanded a lot from them. But, they responded so well and played with great enthusiasm. I stressed teamwork and team unity. I said a prayer standing in a circle with them before every game. It was never a prayer to win. It was a simple prayer asking for God's protection. Many kids, especially those who came from broken homes, grew to like the strict regimen. It included a loving, caring approach, my strange sense of humor and motivational speeches. On several occasions, when we were running late and the umpires were pressuring us to take the field, inevitably one of the kids would always remind me, "Coach Matt, aren't we going to say the team prayer?"

In 1997 I was asked to coach the town's all-star team. We went on to win the class B district championship, winning ten consecutive playoff games. In 1998, we won the very prestigious Class A District All-star championship and made it to the Rhode Island state finals. To me, as much as I enjoyed winning, there was much more at stake. It was about preparing those youths for a world where teamwork, discipline, determination and commitment would become extremely valuable to them. Every boy that ever played for me had to do one thing at the beginning of the season. They had to write their name in black magic marker inside their baseball cap and underneath it write, "NEVER GIVE UP!" That was always our trademark.

Years later, many whom I coached in Little League, that were now in high school and even college, would come up to me and give me a firm handshake and say, "Coach Matt, I still have my hat that says, 'NEVER GIVE UP.'" Or, "Coach Matt, do you remember your old standby Boys to Men speech when we were losing a game?" Or "Hey Coach Matt, I just wanted to thank you for being there for me when my dad wasn't." I will never forget attending a high school varsity tryout, on the day of final cuts, when a young man that I had coached in Little League got cut from the team. By now, he wasn't a kid, well over six feet tall, and 200 lbs. He walked by me, and I could see the look of rejection and sadness in his eyes. As he slowly walked away to his car, I knew exactly what he was feeling.

Making sure no one else was around, I quickly ran over to him and said, "There's always next year, if you want it bad enough, you can do it, I know you can." He immediately burst into tears and gave me a bear hug. The following year, he made the team. Every time I hear positive comments from former team players or run into situations such as those I just described, I get all choked up inside. I count those times as great days of accomplishment in my life. They are life's true nuggets! Days that were fulfilling, and worth writing about. Today, my sons continue to play baseball, one in college and one high school, both have enormous talent. They have both saved many a baseball hat with the words still written in faded black magic marker: "Never Give Up."

With my life changing gears, I began refocusing my time where I thought I was needed most. Without neglecting my career duties or obligations, I started to feel that I was finally, "Getting it!" This was the real meaning of success! For me, there would never be a compromise again, to alter that direction in my life. I also started to feel a need to expand my horizon beyond Rhode Island. I was forty-two years old, but I had the energy of a twenty-two-year-old. I knew I hadn't even scratched the surface of what I wanted to accomplish in my life. I had twelve years of building homes under my belt. It was the longest time that I had ever stuck with one career. For that, I was quite pleased. But I wanted more! It wasn't discontentment! I just wanted to make the most of every day. I wanted the financial freedom and the freedom of my time, to allow me to really live up to my full potential. I wanted to take full advantage of all my God-given talents and not look back when I'm old and gray and wonder, "What if?" I've always had the "Rudy" mentality, you know, from the movie, *Rudy,* about the young man who wanted nothing more than to play football for Notre Dame. He finally realized his dream through relentless determination and desire. I always contend that there's a little Rudy in all of us. We want to believe that we can hang in there, through the battles and set-backs, with sweat and grind, to see our dreams come true. Like Rudy, I had dreams that may have seemed way out of reach to the average Joe. But to me, I had learned by this time in my life, that the only thing that can stop a dream from coming true, is to actually stop believing that it can come true. I was ready at this juncture in my life to aim higher than I ever had, and not give even the slightest thought to, "What if I fail?"

One night in 1998, I lay awake in bed just staring at the ceiling at three o'clock in the morning, as I'd done so many previous times. Margie awakened, opened her eyes, sat up and said to me, "What's going on with you lately? Why are you so restless? What are you thinking about doing now?"

I just stared straight ahead and quietly said, "I believe I'm ready for a new career."

Margie just sort of moaned, said "Good night, Matt," and sank, face first, into her pillow. She knew that we were going on a new journey and knew that it wasn't going to be a cake-walk. But Margie also knew, that when I made my mind up to do something, that I had to give it my all. For me, having her by my side, was all the more reason to try.

*One of my life's treasures — coaching these incredible young men
from Wickford L.L.
My son James, front row, center*

Words of Wisdom

Never Give Up! Write those words down on paper in bold magic marker! Make several copies, and hang them in strategic locations in your home and office. This is just a reminder for you when the going gets rough. It's not the paper, hanging on a wall that will get you through the difficult days. It's the words, embedded in your heart and mind that will help take you through. It's the reminder that you're not alone when you ask the Lord for His help. It's the reminder that you've set out on a mission and pledged to stay the course and have shown the desire and belief in the dream. **Never Give Up,** is the perseverance we talked about for the past twelve chapters. **Never Give Up,** is the spark igniting inside of you. **Never Give Up,** is the lift from the wings of eagles. It's the difference between victory and defeat. You can have moments and times of failure. You can grow weary, and tire, but your relentless determination to get off the mat when you're down is the action that turns dreams into reality. Never give up! Never!

NEVER GIVE UP!

Me, builder of the month,
Builder-Architect Magazine, 1994

*My hero, Uncle Eddie, with my two sons and nephew Jacob Shore
Passover Seder, 1994*

My two favorite girls, Margie and Shayna

Chapter Thirteen

My Great Invention

"Success has nothing to do with what you gain in life or accomplish for yourself. It is what you do for others."
                                        Danny Thomas

If you have an entrepreneurial spirit, you have to learn to live with certain characteristic traits about yourself. For me, being an entrepreneur has always involved taking risk, stepping out, challenging myself, persevering and being able to take the ridicule when the plan doesn't fall right into place. Sometimes, the very characteristic traits that you perceive about yourself as a negative, may in fact, be the driving force behind your great accomplishments. For instance, I'm compulsive and often disorganized. But, I have learned, that while I have to work hard at keeping myself organized and don't often take enough time in doing so, I do put more time into creating ideas and acting on them. So, while I'm always on my own case about getting more organized (and I do work at it) I have learned that my most creative ideas came to me when my desk had three weeks of notes piled up on it. While I have learned that compulsiveness can get me into trouble, it's the same trait that makes me look at an idea and say, "That's it! I'm going for it! It's a done deal, and that's what I want to do."

In 1998, I consciously made up my mind that I was going to go after something that could generate national and perhaps worldwide sales attention. For weeks and months I put ideas on paper. I looked at many options until I decided that I was going to invent something that would have worldwide mass appeal. I didn't have any idea what I was going to invent. I only knew that I was going to invent something. I would watch QVC Network and Home Shopping

Channel for hours at a time, just looking for ideas. I was trying to narrow my invention down to household-type products because they seemed to have the best chance for success and mass appeal. But, I was opened-minded to just about anything that could improve or change the world.

My idea developed in the early winter of 1998. I was meeting my oldest son, Matthew, at his school. He was twelve years old at the time and attended middle school. I was sitting in my truck waiting for him. I spotted him approximately fifty yards away. He saw my truck and started to walk toward me. For the next few minutes I observed his stature. He was bent forward. His arms were straight down by his side and he looked as if he was carrying the weight of the world on his shoulders. When he climbed in the front seat I said, "What are you carrying in your backpack, lead books?"

He just shrugged me off and I took him home. When we got home I took his backpack and weighed it on the bathroom scale. To my disbelief it weighed a tad under thirty-five pounds. I didn't say a word, but my mind was racing a mile a minute. The following morning I quickly offered to drive him to school. Margie looked at me strangely and said, "Be my guest."

When I pulled up to the school, Matt got out of the truck; I quickly yelled out to him, "I'll pick you up."

He just kind of gave me a weird look and said, "Okay, Dad!"

That morning I observed him carefully as he carried his thirty-five- pound backpack into his school. I sat there and carefully analyzed all the other students walking into the school. They were all moving with the same type of load-bearing stride as my son. I whispered to myself, "They all look like they're starring in "Planet of the Apes." One student after another struggled without even realizing it. It was second nature for them to carry twenty-five to forty pounds of weight on their backs. Many were carrying thirty to fifty percent of their own body weight. They did it all day long, in and out of classes. Some carried their load and walked home from school. I just started thinking about the long-term effects on their spine, back, shoulders, and their posture. It wasn't like that for me when I went to school. I carried my books in one arm and left as much as possible in my locker. Yet, these students, including my children, carried their books and seemingly half their belongings inside their backpacks. Why hadn't I noticed it before? It was right in front of me for years. But, I wasn't paying attention!

My mind started to crank into overdrive. I drove to Wal-Mart and purchased a couple of inexpensive backpacks and went right back to my office, closed the door and started to draw pictures. My thought was, if I could come up with a way to distribute the weight inside the backpack and relieve some of the stress and strain on their backs and shoulders and stop these kids from slouching over, I could possibly be on to something huge. I envisioned a rack system that held the books neatly in place inside the backpack. I thought the first place to start was with wood, especially since I had unlimited access to lumber on any given job site. The more I kept toying with the idea the more it started to make sense.

My brother Al's son, Corey, had recently started working for me on the North American Homes construction sites. He was quite the creative young man. I showed him my idea and we started to "toss around" how the rack system could fit in the backpack, hold the books, and distribute the weight at the same time. For the next two weeks we came up with several different designs. Corey kept making prototypes out of plywood and scraps from the job sites. I then took it one step further and purchased a couple of 4'x 8' sheets of polypropylene plastic.

After three weeks of being totally consumed with this project, I had a prototype in my hand that Corey and I thought could do the job. The books slid in on a forty-five-degree angle on three separate shelves. My theory from the beginning was that the side panels of the rack system combined with the horizontal shelf system would work in the same way as a roof truss system where the load is shifted on the side walls of the building or with the same principle of physics involved in a certain type of bridge construction. When a student loaded his backpack on the shelf system, the weight would now be distributed to the side panels rather than dropping like dead weight to the bottom of the bag. It was just the type of invention that I was searching for, and it had the potential for national, even worldwide success. It could greatly benefit students all over the world and sell millions of units at the same time.

I just needed the right design, along with a plan to bring the problem to the surface. I wanted to warn both parents and students alike of the potential risks at hand carrying so much weight, unorganized and undistributed, and in their backpacks, while kids are still growing and in the early developmental stage of their lives. I had one minor problem. I didn't know how to accomplish this task. So I did what I do best. What anyone with a dream must do, I plunged ahead. With my half-wood, half-plastic rack system in hand, my next step was to have some prototype backpacks made. With that, I visited a local sail and canvas maker. Within a few weeks I had a backpack that was customized to hold my rack system. Then I made an appointment with a company called Custom Design, with a very large facility, located in the old Quonset Naval Base Industrial Park not far from my home. It was this appointment that helped to crank my project into second gear.

With my makeshift rack system backpack, I boldly walked into the office of Raul Dias, president and CEO of Custom Design. Raul was a chain-smoking, no-nonsense, type of guy who had his own interpretation and application of the English language. I placed my backpack on his desk, explained my new invention with a naïve type of excitement and enthusiasm. When I was through, he looked at me, leaned back in his big leather chair, put his feet up on his desk, squinted his eyes, kind of turned his head sideways, took a long drag from his cigarette and said sarcastically, "You really want to do this?"

I knew, at that moment, he thought that I was some strange character who was totally off the wall, and was wasting his valuable time. I quickly responded, "I'm positive I want to do this. Can you help me? The rack needs to be made from a durable, flexible, lightweight plastic."

Raul responded with a half chuckle, "Yeah, I can help you."

After, I had been calling him for four consecutive days, Raul finally said to me, "Come on down, I made up a rough prototype for you that I think is going to work."

I arrived at his office and his attitude took a 180-degree turn. He quickly and enthusiastically said to me, "Check this out!" He handed me my backpack with a new shiny black plastic rack system neatly placed inside. "Now, here's how we're going to attach it in the backpack."

While we were discussing the rack system, his two teenage children just happened to walk into his office. They were just getting out of school. He looked over to his daughter and gestured with his hands, "Take your books out of your backpack and put them in Mr. Olerio's backpack."

I quickly showed her how the books neatly stacked on each shelf. She loaded it to the max, zipped it up and threw it over her back. "Oh, my God," she said with a great big smile, "This is so cool, and it feels so much lighter on my back!"

That's all Raul had to hear. For the next thirty days, he became my biggest advocate, as he dove headfirst into my project. His facility spanned well over forty thousand square feet and he employed close to two hundred people. But, all he seemed to have on his mind was my backpack. We spent countless hours together and quickly became great friends. He realized that I was no longer some crazy guy off the street living in fantasy land.

While sitting around the dinner table one night, I was anxious to come up with the right name for my new invention. We were all throwing out crazy names and laughing when all of a sudden my ten-year-old nephew, John, who happened to be dining with us, chimed in and said, "Hey, Uncle Matt, how about calling it the Rak Pak?"

We all looked at each other, shook our heads and said, "That's it, Rak Pak!"

During this time period, I had also researched patent attorneys. It was highly recommended that I go out of state to a firm called Littman Law Offices in Washington, DC. I educated myself as quickly as possible about the various types of patents and trademark laws. I learned that the basic patents to obtain were utility patents and design patents. Utility patents were issued to someone who invented a new product, changed or dramatically improved an existing product, or came up with a new process or method, (a business process, computer process) or chemical composition (new drug). For example, under the utility patent category, there could be a new business process/function on the Internet. In my case, I was issued a patent for my Rakgear Backpack with an internal frame, to evenly distribute books and related items for school students. My patent is registered with the U.S. Patent and Trademark Office as Patent #5,988,476 Rack System for Backpack. Regarding design patents, they are generally issued to someone making a definitive physical or cosmetic change to an existing product. Example: The electric guitar, Flying V shape, is a definite design change to an existing design and would qualify for a design patent. For those of you with patentable ideas, refer to the U.S Patent Office web site at …www.uspto.gov …. Another great reference guide is the book; <u>Patent it Yourself,</u> by David Pressman.

I went through the normal patent search and trademark search procedure, met my financial obligations with Littman Law, and before long, I was on my way to "Patent Pending" status as my invention met the criteria to be patented as a utility patent originally under the trademark name, Rak Pak. Just as with everything else I had ever done in my life, as soon as I started forging ahead and had a definitive plan, the pieces of the puzzle quickly fell into place.

My next idea was to obtain a medical or health care endorsement of some sort. I started with individual doctors, chiropractors and physical therapists, but quickly came to the conclusion that an organization would carry a lot more clout than one or two individual endorsements. I set up an appointment with the governing body of the Rhode Island State Chiropractic Association. After a lengthy conversation with the association president and showing him my invention, he arranged for me to attend an upcoming meeting with the entire board of directors and state members.

The big night came for me to address the Rhode Island Chiropractic Association. With my backpack in hand, neatly put together from Raul's latest prototype rack system, along with a very cool "Rak Pak" logo embroidered on it by a company just a few miles from my home, I proudly walked into the packed meeting of chiropractors. I had several school books with me and had asked my two sons to come along with me as models. I also brought a traditional backpack and filled it with a pile of old school books. I had purposely asked my son, James, to make sure that it weighed exactly thirty pounds, the equivalent to what I had in my Rak Pak. The meeting started. I enthusiastically shared my story and discovery while routinely picking my oldest son up at school, thus, my invention, and my patent pending status from the U.S. Patent Agency. I then unzipped my Rak Pak, with overwhelming OOOhs and AHHs of excitement from the crowd, as seven large test books sat neatly displayed on the three shelves at a forty-five degree angle. It was like I had just unveiled a load of mellow peaches on Park Avenue. I had them eating out of my hands. I had my son Matthew model the traditional sagging backpack with all the books piled in at the bottom. I had my other son, James, model the revolutionary new Rak Pak. I went through my entire thesis on even weight distribution, and how children, in their early skeletal development stages, were at risk. When they carried thirty to forty percent of their body weight in the traditional backpacks, it could be causing irreversible damage to children's postures and spines. I opened up the floor for their opinions, comments, and input on the subject. I had the undivided attention of every chiropractor in the room and the meeting was going better than I could have imagined.

All of a sudden, one of the senior board members stood up and asked if he could feel the contents in each backpack, my Rak Pak and the traditional backpack that James had filled and weighed before we left our home. The senior member held both bags individually and then together, looked at his colleagues and then looked over to me and said, "I believe you're misleading us just a bit, the weight in this traditional backpack seems quite a bit more." I turned beet red and looked over at James now wishing I hadn't trusted a ten-year-old to follow my instructions of placing exactly thirty pounds of books in the bag. With that, another member quickly stood up and shouted, "Let's weigh the two, there's a scale right in my office."

The two gentlemen took both backpacks and left the conference room. I braced myself for the worst as the excitement in the room had quickly changed to an eerie quiet. Five minutes seemed liked an hour. I could feel the sweat running down my forehead. The two men finally emerged back into the room. The senior member held up both bags, and with a big grin shouted, "I was wrong! They're both thirty pounds, on the button." The crowd broke out into laughter and applause. I turned and gave a big smile to James. The remainder of the meeting was open discussion on my future plans for manufacturing, how I would use their endorsement if they were to allow it, and what my marketing and PR plans were to make parents and students aware of my revolutionary product. Then they asked me to leave my Rak Pak with them for four weeks, to conduct their own tests and research and said that they would get back to me with their decision at the next board meeting.

Four weeks and a day from our meeting, I received a phone call from the Rhode Island Chiropractic Association president. He stated,

"After hearing the input and comments from the one hundred seven members and results back from our own tests, the board of directors voted unanimously to endorse the Rak Pak. Congratulations!"

I said, "Thank you, sir!" I hung up the phone and picked up Margie in my arms. Her feet came off the floor as I spun her all around the kitchen. We laughed and were filled with a new sense of excitement and determination.

During that four-week period, Corey and I were also busy working on some cool backpack designs and color combinations. Corey was a computer whiz and used his creativity to develop some very cool Rak Pak logos, hang tags, and brochures. In the meantime, I worked on the text for the hang tags and brochure, and applied for my UPC bar code number for retail sales. I purchased a 1-800 number from the phone company and incorporated the name Wickford Backpack Company, named after a quaint historical section in my home town. I also started to look into manufacturing overseas and was still very busy with Raul working on the next-generation rack system, putting our plans in motion to manufacture a stainless steel mold that could mass produce our racks. The plan was to make the actual backpack overseas and assemble the racks in the bags in Rhode Island. Raul generously offered his facility to assemble the racks until I found a place of my own.

While all of this was taking place, and my life was now moving into overdrive, I still had North American Homes to consider and needed to stay on top of the day-to-day operations as much as possible. Money was starting to become a factor. All of the funding for my new project was coming out of my personal savings. My funds were depleting rapidly as each week passed. The new stainless steel mold alone was a whopping $37,500. The patent attorney fees were quickly adding up. My sample and prototype expenses were through the roof. By this time, I had turned down at least five custom home jobs because I didn't want any interference or distractions while I was pursuing my new dream.

Meanwhile, back on the home front, Margie knew that I was going full speed ahead with my backpack invention, and like everything else I had ever attempted in my life, she was behind me 110%. She just didn't want me to lose sight of putting food on the table and paying our bills. Sometimes you can get so wrapped up in the dream, that you lose sight of the basic necessities of life. In my case, I had been down this road before and I knew I had to make sure that I was still providing for my family spiritually, emotionally, and financially. Margie was seeing our personal bills pile up and was receiving the late-notices in our mail and phone calls. There was a natural, stressful reaction in my wife. She began to worry and be concerned about the money, or the lack of it. But, I have always been a blessed man. I have a wife by my side with a deep faith. In some of our most intense moments she would often say to me, "The Lord will provide" or "God is in control." Sometimes I would have to remind her of this by using those same words. I knew I was going to make something big happen. I knew God was with me. I just wasn't sure **when** it would happen. That's where the perseverance comes in. That's where the faith factor comes in. That's when you take out the baseball cap that says, "Never Give Up!" Don't ever forget that you and your spouse are a team. A team needs to communicate and build each other up during the tough times.

Besides all the bills piling up, I also ran into a stone wall. I received a phone call from my trademark patent attorney. He said, "Rak Pak is out! Change the name to something else. It's too close to another product name that we recently discovered. You can chance it, but I don't think you want to go down that road."

After two days of agonizing over the name change, I changed the name to Rak Sak. I didn't like it as much, but it seemed to work.

I researched various options for materials to use for our first round of manufacturing and learned about denier (the durability labeling of nylon material) and buckles, zippers and webbing, foam padding and zipper pulls, and shoulder straps. I spent a lot of time at Bryant College Import Export Center and hooked up with a nice lady named, Ana Morgan. Ana was from El Salvador. She spoke fluent Spanish and took an immediate interest in my project. I had been reading up on the North American Free Trade Agreement [NAFTA] and had made several phone calls to Mexico, starting with the U.S Embassy. They pointed me in the right direction, supplying me with a list of backpack manufacturers in Mexico City and the surrounding areas. After learning that a backpack was called a *mochilla* in Spanish, I made some wild phone calls to Mexico as Margie listened, with hysteria, in the background. "Hello, do you speak English? Hello, senorina, I'm calling from America. Hello, mochillas, I want to speak to someone about making mochillas, hello! Hello? Hello?"

With most phone calls the response was usually the same. "Oh, mochillas... si, si senor," and then a rambling of Spanish and the phone would click off.

My persistence paid off. I finally connected with a gentleman named Alberto, who spoke English and understood exactly what I wanted to accomplish. I sent him my prototype backpacks with drawings of various new design ideas. He priced out the labor to manufacture, but stated that I would have to supply the material. In Mexico at the time, it was very difficult for them to get their hands on premium material, like 1000 denier nylon, which was made in the U.S. and used in many of the top brand-name backpacks such as Jansport and Eastpak. I found what I was looking for at a company in California. I had rolls of the material trucked right to Alberto's factory in Mexico City. Meanwhile, Ana Morgan from Bryant College had called me and mentioned that she was taking a trip to Mexico the following week and asked if she could assist me in any way. I asked her if she would be willing to visit Alberto's factory and make sure he understood everything that was discussed over the phone. She graciously agreed.

Everything was falling into place. Ana came back from Mexico the following week with preliminary samples from Alberto. They were a bit rough around the edges, but not bad for the first round. I contacted Alberto, we made some adjustments and within two weeks I had twelve pretty cool-looking samples in various colors. Ana, in the meantime, mentioned a connection that she had with Channel Ten News, Health Reporter, Barbara Morse. Barbara was very popular on the Rhode Island news scene. She liked what she was hearing about my invention and agreed to interview me. She showed up at my door a few days later complete with camera crew and microphone in hand. My home was filled with my family, my son's friends, Corey, and Ana. Barbara and I hit it off right away. Her warm personality and charm made me feel comfortable right from the start. She absolutely loved the "Rak Sak" and spent over an hour filming, interviewing me, then Corey, my sons and their friends. She left as excited as we were.

The following day, Barbara Morse called me on the phone. She said, "You're on tonight at six and eleven. Make sure you're watching!" By 6:00 P.M. everyone in my family, including my mom and dad and half the kids in the neighborhood, were packed into our family room in front of our TV set. Margie's family, my brothers, sister, aunts and uncles were all notified of the big event. Six P.M. came and there was Barbara Morse on television standing next to me, showing off the Rak Sak. She was incredible. It seemed almost as though it was her invention. She was proud as a peacock as she started in with a big smile and a voice filled with enthusiasm. She said, "Let me tell you about an invention that's going to revolutionize the backpack industry. It's called the Rak Sak, designed by a Rhode Island man, named Matt Olerio."

We went wild. Everyone was screaming and jumping up and down like little kids in our family room. She went on, "The Rak Sak's patented even weight distribution rack system was designed to distribute all that weight that your children are carrying in their backpack. It is proudly endorsed by the Rhode Island Chiropractic Association because of its unique ability to help relieve stress and strain on a student's back, spine and shoulders. It also helps to improve their carrying posture. Besides all that, it also keeps your books and papers neat and organized."

The segment then switched to an interview with me, then Corey, and some children from the neighborhood. She methodically showed the viewers how to stack each book on the shelves, showed off the cool logo and organizational features. She ended the segment by saying, "I'm quite sure that you're going to want to know how to order a Rak Sak. I know that I'm going to want one for myself. Just call Wickford Backpack Company at 1-800-RAK-7705." Then the 800 number appeared on the screen in big, bold numbers and just froze right there for a good five seconds.

We then went into hyper excitement mode as my dad yelled out, "I don't believe it! She just gave you one million dollars worth of free advertisement!" The phone was literally ringing off the hook from family and friends. We walked on cloud nine for the remainder of the evening. We tuned in for the 11:00 P.M. segment, as well. I was now certain that the Rak Sak had all the makings of a grand slam. I just needed to figure out how I was going to take it to the next level and what I was going to do when I ran out of money!

MELLOW PEACHES, THREE POUNDS FOR A DOLLAR

I was sitting in my office two days after the Barbara Morse report, when all of a sudden my fax machine clicked on by the side of my desk. It was an order for two Rak Saks from a woman in Corpus Christi, Texas. My 800# line was tied directly into a full-service agency that offered twenty-four-hour customer service. It was a bit expensive, but I wanted to take a professional approach from the start in handling phone orders. I looked at the order and smiled to myself figuring someone in Rhode Island saw the news clip and ordered these for a relative living in Texas. The day before I had received approximately 350 orders from Rhode Islanders watching the segment. Within a few minutes, another order came in from Savannah, Georgia for three Rak Saks and then another from Paramus, New Jersey for two more. All of a sudden, like something out of an "I Love Lucy" episode, my fax machine starting spitting out orders in nonstop succession from all over the country. I'm not talking about a few orders. I'm talking about orders coming out as fast as the fax machine could spit them out. I just sat there in disbelief. I kept loading the fax machine with paper. Then my phone rang. It was a news reporter from Atlanta. She was asking if I would be willing to give her an interview about my Rak Sak backpack. I said, in a dumbfounded voice, as I looked over at my fax machine which was working in overdrive, "What's going on? How did you get my name and number?" She replied, as if I was living in the boondocks, "Haven't you heard? Your story about the Rak Sak was picked up on two hundred NBC affiliate stations on the news feed from NBC News Health Check with Barbara Morse."

I sat back in my chair in disbelief. Then, I called Margie, speaking to her a mile a minute, filled with excitement! I called my dad, who had just returned to Florida. I said, "You think that onions, five pounds for a dollar, generated action? Wait until you hear this one!"

Twelve hours later, I took stock of one of the craziest days in my life and just stared at the piles and piles of orders spread out all over my desk and on the floor. By midnight, there were over four thousand orders placed from Hawaii to Alaska to Miami and everywhere else in between, all paying $49.95 plus $7.95 shipping and handling, for a backpack they saw for less than three minutes on an NBC Health Watch segment from Rhode Island. I went to bed, not thinking about a grand slam anymore, I was thinking, "This is going to be bigger than I ever imagined!"

Motivation vs. Passion and Desire

Listening to an inspiring motivational speaker, whether live or through audio tape, or reading motivational/self-help material, can certainly be uplifting, inspiring, and extremely beneficial when pursuing your dreams. However, that is where it ends. The passion, desire, and plan of action need to take over. I remember several years ago a Rhode Island boxer from my hometown, named Vinny Pazienza, watched the movie, *Rocky*, when it first came to the movie theaters. It moved him and inspired him to a point where he eventually went on to win three world boxing titles in three different weight classes. Was he motivated by the movie and the infamous *Rocky* theme that sent chills down your spine? You bet he was! But the movie didn't make his hands faster and his jab more effective. It didn't make his knockout punch more powerful or increase his stamina to go twelve rounds. That was developed from pure sweat, hard work, a solid game plan, and a good trainer. Motivational speeches, audio tapes, movies, and literature offer great jump starts for the mind, but the truth is, they have no staying power. They have no shelf life. It is the desire to achieve and accomplish something extraordinary that adds fuel to the fire and sets your dream in motion. It is the physical act of doing something and making those motivational words come alive in you. Great words without action on your part are left as just… great words.

I can stand in an auditorium and deliver a powerful, inspirational speech on pursuing your greatest goals. I might ignite a life-changing spark in you that soon turns into all-out rocket fuel and you might leave that auditorium pumped up and ready to take on the world. But, now comes the hard part when you have to wake up the next morning and the rubber hits the road. Your bills are piling up, and the daily toils and struggles of life set in and take over. Remember my great speech? It's not cutting it any longer unless you took action on the words. I certainly could have said something that set that desire into first gear. But no speech can propel you into second gear, third or overdrive. That has to come from within, and it is there that you will find just how determined and focused you really are. You'll see results when you'll finally say to yourself, "No more excuses. I'm putting my plan into action and there's just no stopping me!"

Rakgear Backpacks — Internal Frame, U.S. Patent 59988476

Chapter Fourteen

I Did It My Way… But I had a Whole Lot of Help!

"A family is a place where principles are hammered and honed on the anvil of everyday living."
                                                        Charles R.. Swindoll

Throughout my life of embarking upon several great adventures and pursuing my dreams, I have learned, unequivocally, to surround myself with good, honest, reliable, dedicated, loyal people. I strongly suggest that you do the same. I don't think you will ever hear someone who has gone on to reach extraordinary heights in their lives, say, that they did it all on their own. Even Frank Sinatra, who sang the smash hit "My Way," knew it took help to do it his way. Have you ever watched the "Up Front and Personal" segments of the Olympic Games? While they're playing that long standing, memorable, Olympic theme in the background, the most gifted athletes humbly pay tribute to their coaches and family members, time and time again. They often say, "If it wasn't for so and so, I never would have accomplished my goals and dreams." I'm quite sure that there is no such thing as, "Going it alone." At least not in my book!

As my newly formed backpack company started to take off like a rocket ship, I immediately recognized the need to surround myself with quality people. I immediately recognized that I had an entourage of support. Besides having my wife behind me 110% (this, for me, has always made all the difference in the world), I had my nephew Corey, who was extremely creative and a hard-working young man. I had Ana Morgan, who was relentless when it came to research and getting into, seemingly, closed doors. There was Raul Dias, who at our first meeting looked at me as if I had two heads. But, he soon became a great friend, advisor, and was instrumental in developing the first-generation rack systems. I had Littman Law offices, who, although they were not working with me on a day-to-day basis, knew the ins and outs of, not only obtaining a patent, but also of how to avoid needless lawsuits and heartache. I had my five brothers and one sister and their children from whom I could bounce ideas off, and seek advice. I had my dad, who, though older and mellower, still provided me with day-to-day advice via telephone and kept a very strong interest in me every step of the way. My dad would often say to me, at this point in my life, "You know, better than I do, I can't really offer you business advice any more." The truth is, a father's wisdom is invaluable when you are in the midst of doing battle. I also had my mom for continuous love and support. I had aunts, uncles and cousins that built me up and bragged about me as if I had just invented a state-of-the-art nuclear submarine. I had my children to help keep me on course and bring me down to earth like only they know how to do. I had my brothers-in-law, Jim and Mark, at my disposal. They offered words of wisdom to help enhance my product line. My seven wonderful sisters-in-law, always came through with the right words, at the right time. I had great neighbors and friends, who were more like family, and took a vested interest in everything that I was doing. I even had my mother-in-law, who constantly reminded me that, "Behind every great man there is an even greater woman." There was also another man who proved to be one of the driving forces behind me, and that was my accountant, Paul. I grew up with Paul. I went through school with him. He was even there to support me back in the days during the big showdown at City Hall, when I was on Park Avenue selling fruit and produce. He is a gifted accountant. But even more so, he's an organizational genius. Paul is so organized that even his visits to the bathroom are, "By appointment only." He was just the opposite of me. I used to drive him up a wall, but we worked well together. His dedication, wisdom, and inspiration to Wickford Backpack Company were invaluable. He put together my initial business plan, did all our cost analysis, set up the new corporation, handled the books, bank accounts and acted as a middle man in handling most of the company's dispute issues. As we grew, it was his participation, business skills, and friendship that provided the stability that was needed to go to the next level.

    It's so important to recognize those who support you, stick by your side. They encourage you, and offer much needed wisdom. They are the ones who often go unnoticed when you finally reach the pinnacle of your goals and dreams.

Chapter Fifteen

From Rak Sak...to...Rakgear to China?

"Were it offered to my choice, I should have no objections to a repetition of the same life from its beginning, only asking the advantages authors have in a second edition to correct some faults of the first."

Ben Franklin

By early 1999, Wickford Backpack Company and the Rak Sak were in high gear. Looking back on what followed after that miracle day in my office, when over four thousand backpack orders came in via the fax, it seemed like a fairy tale, but not without a few big, bad, wolves along the way. After miraculously filling all the orders that came in and shipping them out in individual boxes from Raul's factory, we barely broke even. I knew that I needed to start making good, sound, prudent, decisions. That's what we focused on as a team. By this time, I had stopped my building business altogether. I had all, but depleted my savings to fund our personal living expenses, Wickford Backpack's manufacturing, research & development, and payroll. In the winter of 1999, we had filmed a commercial and hired a marketing firm to design our hang tags, brochures, advertisement copy, and press releases. By this time, the Rak Sak had appeared and was featured on CNN News, ABC News, Good Morning America and several prominent magazines and newspapers throughout the United States and Canada. It was being dubbed as the new and safe way for students to carry their books.

Desperately needing a major influx of working capital, and knowing that I was draining my financial resources to dangerous levels, Paul and I set out to find Venture Capital. Time was of the essence! We needed to keep up the locomotive-like momentum that we had behind us. Out of the blue, a former homebuilding customer referred me to an attorney who was said to have the ways and means to hook us up with an honest/reliable venture capitalist. Within just two weeks of our initial meeting, I had met with the venture principals and had a contract in hand to raise the necessary funds. There was only one catch. If I could not meet the deadlines of the note, I would forfeit 50% of Wickford Backpack, including my patent. With our backs against the wall, Paul and I, along with my dad, came to the conclusion that this was the only way that we knew of to take the Rak Sak to the next level. The clincher for me, to sign on the dotted line, was the available factory and office space they offered to us. One of their many businesses consisted of a lace company. It was located just twenty minutes from my home, in a turn-of-the-century textile mill that spanned seventy-two thousand square feet, complete with two loading docks. We were immediately offered approximately thirty thousand square feet of factory and office space. The space was perfect and met all our needs. Within three weeks' time, we were ready to set up shop and bring containers in from Asia. I signed on the dotted line, and Wickford Backpack Company was now, officially, set up to do business in large volume and effectively ship it out anywhere in the country.

While participating in one of the largest retail tradeshows in the world, called SHOPA, in Atlanta, and setting up our own RAK SAK booth, I started to make some important connections with retail buyers from some of the largest retail chains in the country. My Rak Sak was a genuine show stopper and our booth was nonstop action. We even placed second in the best new product category out of hundreds of entries throughout the United States. Across the aisle from my booth, was an up and coming company called Glacier Gear/ CD Projects which was under the corporate name, Roundhouse. They were much larger in sales volume than Rak Sak. They were in their fifth year of business, and their booth, which was three times larger than mine, also had nonstop action. On the last day of the show, I introduced myself to the company's founder and president. They happened to be selling off their samples to other show attendees. This is customary for many vendors to do on the last day of a trade show. I was so impressed by their designs, materials and color combinations. I proceeded to purchase every last sample that they were offering to sell. Just like so many other times in my life, I got the same strange look of bewilderment as the Glacier Gear folks just gawked at me. I dragged away two huge boxes overflowing with their lunch bags, cooler bags, and CD cases. My flight home arrived in at one o'clock in the morning. Besides my luggage, I had managed to fly home with two oversized boxes of merchandise. I immediately went into my garage and ripped open my stash of bags. With everyone sound asleep, I proceeded to line up every Glacier Gear Lunch bag and cooler bag on the shelves in my garage. When I was done, I just stood back and stared at them. In the meantime, Margie woke up. She opened the garage door that leads into the house, and saw all the bags on the shelves, and me staring at them. She said with her eyes half closed, "Now what are you up to?"

I just turned and said, "I'm changing the name tomorrow from Rak Sak to Rakgear; what do you think?"

Margie rolled her eyes and said, "That's great, Matt! Do you know what time it is?" I said, "Don't you get it, "Glacier gear ....Rakgear, it's a much cooler/hipper name than Rak Sak!"

I cleared the name with Littman law offices. Within two weeks, we were officially Rakgear. With our new factory in place, new name, great press, newfound venture capital, and an incredible trade show experience and exposure, I was only looking in one direction. Up! Straight to the top! Within a few weeks, I made plans to go to Hong Kong and mainland China to visit a new factory. I had established a business relationship with them a few months earlier. Going to China was an eye-opening experience for me. I had been to Haiti twice before, volunteering and designing a new septic system for a school in Port-au-Prince. As overwhelming as Haiti was to me, as far as poverty and depravation, China just blew my mind with the number of people, the lack of infrastructure, and lack of air pollution regulations. There were people in mass quantities everywhere. The streets were chaotic, with a combination of motorcycles, motor scooters, bicycles, taxis, and horse-drawn carts, with horns blasting continually. The air was so thick, so polluted in Guang Zhou, China (pronounced Guan Jo), that my eyes were constantly irritated and my throat was parched. The Chinese people, however, were extremely friendly and cordial. Being a 6'3" tall American also made me stand out in the crowd, whether I wanted to or not. I ate snake, chicken feet, fish eye soup, and literally everything else imaginable. The food was challenging, to say the least, but I loved the people and the culture. When I arrived at the factory, it was an old decrepit, large, three story building. When I stepped out of the taxi, there was a contingent of Chinese factory managers waiting for me, shaking my hands, bowing, and smiling. Within ten seconds, a barrage of firecrackers went off ten feet from me, and everyone started to cheer. They pointed at me to look up. On the third floor there were hundreds of Chinese men and women hanging out the windows smiling and waving and pointing to a thirty-foot-long, bright red sign that said, "Welcome Matt Olerio."

I had already shipped approximately eighteen thousand backpacks from their factory to my factory in Rhode Island. They wanted to show their appreciation for my business.

Before entering into mainland China, I had stayed in Hong Kong. Someone from my church had asked me if I would look up the International Bible League while I was out there. They supplied me with the name of an American living in Hong Kong. Sitting in my hotel room one evening, I made the call. The gentleman was cordial and excited to hear from another American. After some small talk, he learned that I would be entering into mainland China within a few days. He became quite enthusiastic. He asked me if I would be willing to carry through customs a large trunk weighing two hundred pounds filled with Bibles (an illegal book in mainland China). My initial reaction was a dumfounded, "Uh...I'm here on business! I don't think I can do that for you! Besides, I'll be traveling with a few other Chinese businessmen that will be meeting me at the train station. I don't think I could explain away a two hundred pound trunk filled with Bibles, and risk being caught, attempting to carry it over the border."

He quietly said, "Well, think about it! I'll be praying for you and I'll call you the day before you leave for the mainland."

We said goodbye, and I felt relieved. The following day, the two gentlemen that were supposed to accompany me, called and said that their plans had changed. They would not be able to join me. Instead, they would make arrangements for a chaperone to meet me, once I crossed over and went through customs. Now I was thinking, "There goes that excuse! This guy must have been praying long and hard."

Sure enough, he called the next day. I agreed to do it. He laid out the entire plan over the phone. The last thing he said was, "God bless you! Be careful!"

When I arrived at the train station in Hong Kong the next morning, I was to look for a rather robust gentleman with white hair. He would have the trunk. As the final boarding call was given at the train station, there was still no sign of my drop-off man. I felt a bit relieved and was quite eager to board the train empty handed. All of a sudden, I turned my head and there he was standing six feet behind me. He quickly shook my hand, smiled and said, "Hi Matt, long time no see." He walked away leaving this enormous stainless steel trunk by my side.

I quickly gave a few looks to my right and left as if I were in some espionage movie, grabbed the trunk, and dragged it inside the train. With every last ounce of energy I could muster, I somehow managed to get it over my head and up into the overhead compartment above my seat. I turned around to sit down. I couldn't help but notice that every eye on that overcrowded train was on me. As it is, I'm a 6'3", 225 pound American, and now, carrying a huge trunk. I just sat down, looked up, and said to myself. "How am I ever going to get that trunk down from there without it smashing to the ground and busting open?"

And then, the realty set in. I had to take that trunk through the very strict mainland China Customs, which was about a three-hour train-ride away. Besides the fact that they frowned on Americans, to some degree, entering their country, I had the double whammy, with a 200 pound trunk full of illegal Bibles!

I arrived in Guang Zhou and stared out the window as the train slowly entered the station and Republic of China Customs. Like something out of a World War II movie, I saw a row of Chinese soldiers about the length of a football field, spaced twenty feet apart along the railroad tracks. They were dressed in bright green army fatigues, each standing at attention, brandishing a submachine gun across his chest with his eyes fixed straight ahead. They were like mannequins. I just took a deep breath, wondered what I had gotten myself into, and just whispered under my breath, "Here we go, Matt."

I somehow managed to get the trunk down. I climbed off the train, tried not to look or act suspicious, and got into the line to officially enter China. I had fifteen or so customs agent lines to choose from, and just picked one randomly. As my turn came up in line, wouldn't you know it, I had to deal with the most miserable customs agent in China. I knew baggage searches were random and that's all that I was thinking about. He looked at me with a sour expression and blurted out in broken English, "You fill out visa paperwork wrong; go back to table and then get back in line."

I just politely nodded my head yes; who was I to argue. I immediately saw my mistake on the document, made the correction and then proceeded back to the line. As my sweat was visibly dripping down my forehead, all that went through my mind was, "Do I really want to get back in this line with Mr. Personality?" But then I was thinking, "Well, if I don't, he might get suspicious." I said a very quick prayer; "Please Lord, show me the right line, You gotta help me out here."

I got back into Mr. Miserable's line and within ten seconds a very tall, well- dressed Chinese gentleman stepped out of line and spoke to me in a very cordial tone. "You don't have to wait in this line. You can go to any other line where there are less people waiting."

That's all I had to hear. I was sure that was a sign to move. I quickly grabbed my trunk. I went all the way to the other end of the building where a young Chinese female customs agent was seated. I said hello, and gave her my best American smile. She stared at my passport and visa. She smiled back at me and stamped my passport. I walked on through, as I observed several customs agents with dogs going through people's luggage. I took one quick glance back in the direction of the tall, polite, Chinese gentleman and smiled to myself thinking, "I believe that man was my angel." I proceeded down a very steep escalator and noticed an American-looking gentleman waiting at the bottom. As I touched down, he came up to me, shook my hand and said, "Hey Matt, long time no see!"

He took the trunk and walked away. I just watched him from a distance and thought to myself, "What a rewarding job he has." Within a few minutes my chaperones showed up and gave me a warm welcome as we hopped into a taxi. They took me out for lunch. I ate snake in a spicy celery broth, fish eye soup, and drank a bottle of Coca-Cola. I was as happy as a clam.

I flew home a few days later with a whole new outlook and an education in manufacturing and dining in the Orient. With the relationships I had firmly established in China, as well as the new backpack designs, I really started to feel that we were headed in the right direction. I had learned the ropes of importing goods from overseas. I had my own customs broker. I used all the negotiation skills that I had learned as a teenager (when I bought produce and flowers) to negotiate with the Chinese businessmen. By now, we had an actual assembly line in our factory; which employed approximately twenty people, ranging from forklift operators, to shippers, to assembly men and women. We were taking in containers from overseas and shipping out thousands of units to many large retailers. But, the sales numbers needed to increase substantially in order to cover our expenses. I had to find a way to sell many more thousands of units. Rakgear had come so far, so fast, and now it was time to see just how far we could go with it. I was living out my dream, to sell products nationwide and worldwide, and was more determined than ever, to see it through to completion.

Me standing next to a security guard in Guang Zhou, China, complete with fireworks and welcome sign

Me and Miguel standing shoulder to shoulder on my first visit to Porto Prince, Haiti

Me and Juan at the gates of Providence Haitian Project, Porto Prince

Chapter Sixteen

Minnesota Can Be a Cold Place

"To win one's joy through struggle is better than to yield to melancholy."
Andre Gide

I never want anyone reading Mellow Peaches to think for a moment, that everything I touched in my life instantly turned into a pot of gold. Quite the contrary, in fact, it would take literally hundreds of pages, if I were to write about all my set backs, frustrations, failures, and feelings of despair associated with all my success stories. The truth is, progression and accomplishments can not be realized without turbulence, mistakes, and at times, questioning your own abilities and talents. It's those very days, filled with doubt and mistakes, that actually allow you to assess your situation, take a better course of action, and come back fighting the next day.

I can remember flying from Rhode Island to Minnesota for an appointment that I had with a retail buyer for Target Stores. I was so proud of myself for even getting the appointment in the first place. I was convinced that I was going to close the deal and have my backpack placed in every Target store across the United States. I purchased my plane tickets, booked a nice hotel, rented a nice car, had on my best suit, and was ready with all my samples and promo to consummate the deal. When I got to Target headquarters, I was escorted into the buyer's office. He looked up at me, gave me a lame hand shake, and said, "Uh, I can only give you three minutes, so you'll have to speak fast."

I went through my spiel, while he kept his eyes fixed on his computer, and never even looked at my backpacks or material. I wanted to tell him off. But instead, I thanked him for his time, left his office, and went back to my hotel room feeling like the biggest fool on the face of the earth. I just sat in my room thinking out loud to myself, "What am I doing? I spent all this money to come out here, and this guy wouldn't give me the time of day, never mind buy my backpacks."

After an hour or so went by, I decided I wasn't going back home until I did something productive. So, I opened up the Yellow Pages and started calling college bookstores in the area to set up appointments for the following day. Instead of selling 15,000 units to Target Stores, I managed to sell 300 units to seven different college bookstores. Was I feeling foolish and disappointed? You bet I was! But I learned a great deal about qualifying my appointments the next time so I could increase my chances of closing the deal. I also learned, that in most cases, when dealing with large retail chain buyers, it is much wiser to employ an established manufacturers' sales rep. who already has an ongoing, long term relationship with the buyer.

No dream worth pursuing is without its down days. It's how we handle the down days that matter. The trip to Minnesota was a disaster. However, for me, going home with 300 units sold was better than going home with nothing sold. I tried to make the best out of a bad situation, sometimes that's all we can do. I also knew that I'd get my chance again with Target Stores, another time, another buyer. I knew that I'd be back again one day, which brings me to another important lesson. Don't burn bridges behind you. Believe me! I'm a big enough guy that I could have taken that buyer's wimpy hand shake, and squeezed his hand so that he would have never forgotten me. But instead, I politely said, "Thank you for your time."

Pursuing your dream can often be discouraging, humbling, and stressful. But the rewards for following through on your dream and staying the course can never be matched.

Margie and James on the set of CBN — 700 Club, 1999

My beautiful family
L-R: Matthew Jr., Me, Shayna, Margie, and James

Chapter Seventeen

The Acquisition

"It is impossible on reasonable grounds to disbelieve miracles."
Blaise Pascal

I often refer to a quote by Walt Disney, "If you can dream it, you can do it." I had a dream to patent an invention and accomplish its worldwide distribution. The dream was the easy part. It's the "you can do it" part of the quote that presents the biggest challenge. Throughout this book I have attempted, through my own experiences and through life's lessons, to teach you that the dream is what starts the making of the blueprint or plan. But, deep down in your heart, you have to believe that YOU CAN DO IT. The dream has to be a true desire of your heart in order for it to take root, grow and blossom. If it is the true desire of your heart, and if you follow many of the basic formulas we have discussed in the previous chapters, you will realize your dream and you will find that the possibilities are endless for you. I don't just write these words. I live these words. You need to live them too and embed them in the depths of your heart.

I realized that Wickford Backpack had to generate a lot more volume to cover our expenses, and also to keep our venture capitalists at bay. It was a new challenge for me. In spite of the rapid and early successes we had achieved, money started to come into play more than ever. Working capital is often the neutralizer in any great venture. You can get all the press in the world and all the hype that money can buy, but at the end of the day, it's what your checkbook says that dictates your course of action. When you're in the middle of doing battle, you're not even thinking of winning the war, you're thinking of getting through the day. For me that battle was a constant, daily struggle for more working capital. With all I had going for me with

Wickford Backpack Company, I could not afford to rest or to let my guard down for one day. We were plowing through money like it was free air that came out of the AC vents. I had dealt with very large sums of money with North American Homes, but usually I had my bank loans to support the projects. This time, I had a fixed amount of venture capital to work with, and when it was gone, it was gone, and so was half of everything I owned, including my patent. By the way, it was finally issued to me in late 1999, almost two years to the date of my application. I was also patented in ninety countries worldwide, quite a far cry from picking my son up from school one day and making plywood racks.

    I just kept surging ahead. I had three successful showings on QVC Network. We managed to get a national endorsement by the Congress of Chiropractic and State Associations, and started to sell thousands of backpacks nationwide, directly to chiropractors. We reached a level, where we had shipped six packs of Rakgear, to over one thousand chiropractic offices, with many of them paying over the phone, using their Visa/Master card. It helped our cash flow; but, it was doing business the hard way. Our national press coverage was going stronger than ever. We also had a feature article in *Girls Life Magazine, Elle Magazine,* and *Healthy Living*. We had countless newspaper articles written on Rakgear. I even appeared on the "700 Club" with Pat Robertson's co-host Terri Meusson . If there was a chance for free publicity touting Rakgear, I was there. Ana lined up a study with Okalahoma State University that actually conducted a four-month experiment on Rakgear's patented, even-weight distribution, rack system. Professor Bert Jacobson led the charge at Oklahoma State, and even presented Rakgear before the American College of Sports Medicine. We not only passed with flying colors and received rave reviews; we wound up being featured in U.S. Journal of Ergonomics. We also worked with a Dr. Pascoe, at Auburn University, to further enhance the ergonomic abilities of Rakgear. We developed contoured shoulder straps based on her expertise from a two-year study that she had conducted, on the adverse effects of backpacks on students. We literally got to a point where we couldn't lift our heads, without someone telling us of another article written about backpack safety. Some related how a student shouldn't carry more than 10-15% of their total body weight on their backs and how most students were carrying

30-40% of their total body weight. Other ergonomic backpacks and related products started to surface. But we felt that, without a doubt, we had brought a national concern into the light. We had single-handedly changed the way parents and students evaluate their backpacks. I felt then, and still do today, that Rakgear revolutionized the backpack industry. We forced the hands of some of the largest backpack manufacturers and distributors in the world to become more accountable for the manufacturing of their packs, adding ergonomic features and comfort for students. I was even invited to address the design and marketing team at the largest backpack manufacturer in the world, Jansport. I gave my presentation at their corporate headquarters in Appleton, Wisconsin, while then CEO, Paul Delorey, and cofounder, Skip Yowell, sat in on the meeting. Rakgear was making its mark and opening doors that I never thought were possible.

However, as well as things were going, money was still the ongoing concern. In the late summer of 1999, I was forced to sell 50% of my company to the venture capital group along with 50% of my patent. I just couldn't hold on any longer. I didn't look at it as a setback. I saw it as an opportunity to go to yet another level. Besides, 50% of something, is a lot better than 100% of nothing. I still controlled the day-to-day operations of the company. I now had the needed working capital to move forward, and actually had their wisdom and expertise at my disposal. Things were going very well as I continued to get more and more positive press for our products and make more and more connections for retail sales. By now, I had a national network of manufacturer sales reps, geographically positioned throughout the United States and Canada. Our designs were dramatically improving. I expanded my product line to include an ergonomic diaper bag called "Baby Rakgear." We also created a paintball vest called "Cobra Gear." Our preschool backpack was called "Lit'l Locker!" Our rolling backpack was called the "Rakgear Travel Pak!" Our lightweight biking/hiking pack was called the "Rakgear Vest Pak."

I also landed an enormous retail account after I came up with a game plan/strategy. I presented it to one of the senior VP's at CVS Pharmacy, the second largest drug store chain in the United States. The backpack buyer for CVS had turned me down. He said that CVS could never sell a backpack for $40, even if it did the kids' homework for them. He adamantly insisted that the most they could sell a backpack for was $14.95 and with that, our meeting was officially over. I'm not one to take "no" for an answer so easily. I went over his head, and wrote to the CEO. Within one week of writing my letter, I ended up getting an appointment with the senior VP of Marketing. When it was all said and done, we shipped a display and backpack with order coupons to all 4,500 CVS stores nationwide. It was the first time that they had ever allowed such a phenomenon to take place in their stores. The plan allowed for their customers to actually order a Rakgear backpack off a corrugated display sitting in each store by filling out an order coupon, pre- paying it to a CVS clerk, followed by the clerk or manager faxing the order to us in Rhode Island. We would, in turn, drop ship the pack directly to the customer's home and handle all customer service related questions on our end. It was almost as good an idea as selling onions five pounds for a dollar and tulips for $2.99, all rolled into one. For me, it was an incredible accomplishment, especially when the orders came rolling through the fax machines every morning.

The more Rakgear backpacks we sold, the more letters we received from satisfied customers. I had accumulated literally hundreds of letters from students all over the country commenting and thanking me for my invention. They expressed how their Rakgear backpacks had helped their backs and made them more organized. I was so proud, and felt so blessed to have come so far in such a short time. But, as so many times before in my life, stone walls appeared and unforeseen setbacks knocked at my door.

That's just what happened the week after Christmas in 1999. I received a call from the venture capital group attorney. He told me that there was a falling out among the group and some key figures were parting ways. He stated that they would be putting the brakes on Rakgear. They had sunk well over 1.5 million dollars into Rakgear. The member who was the biggest supporter and number-one fan was leaving the group. The remaining members had no interest in the project. They didn't see it as one of their powerhouses. So, all bets were now off. "Hasta la vista!" No more money! I had the option to either buy them out or fund it, from that point on, with my own money. I was upset, shocked, and disappointed! But I didn't feel like the end was near. I put my head down and kept pushing ahead. Paul and I put our heads together to come up with as many ideas as possible to buy them out. By April of 2000, the money was drying up, and each phone call from Paul became more and more alarming, with more and more urgency in his voice. We both knew that we had to do something. Paul kept repeating the urgency to make more money and put in more money or it was just a matter of time before the doors would close. I pumped as much of my personal money as I could into the company, but to no avail. I went home one night in April 2000 feeling that the dream may in fact be coming to an end. For the first time I was actually thinking that this could be it. We needed too much money. I lay awake in bed staring at the ceiling. Margie knew it was eating away at me. I looked at her and said, "Look what I did to us again. I'm chasing a dream at an age when I should have been content with what I was. No…, I had to be Matt, the dream chaser."

Margie looked at me and said what she had said so many times before, "Did you ask God for help? Did you bring it before Him?"

I looked at her and said "I have, but maybe not the way I should have."

Margie always said, "The sunrise brings new hope and His mercies are new every morning." I woke up the next morning. I prayed, put on my baseball cap that said "NEVER GIVE UP." I contacted a company that specialized in putting together corporate business plans. They assist companies in raising capital through bond offerings or buyouts. It was very expensive, but it had to be done. We needed a top-notch professional business plan. The other plan that I put into overdrive, I had been pursuing for months. It was an elephant-size account to sell backpacks. But I just couldn't get passed second base with the buyer. I decided that I was going to pull out all the stops and use every salesmanship skill that I had ever learned. The company I targeted was Walgreens. I had figured, if I landed the number two drug store chain in the country, why not go after the number one chain.

By mid-April, it happened. My persistence and determination had paid off. The Walgreens buyer faxed a purchase order for twenty-four thousand units of Rakgear backpacks. It was, by far, the single largest order that we had received to date, worth over a half-million dollars in revenue. Now, with the purchase order in my hand, I had one real big problem, I needed over $300,000 to manufacture and ship the backpacks to them. In the position we were in, it may as well have been three million dollars. But, there is one thing I had learned from my teenage years: where there's a will, there's a way. When there is prayer, there is always hope.

   I remembered two very important things at that moment in my life. The first came to me as I walked out into the factory and unzipped one of the backpacks. From inside of it I pulled out one of the thousands of bookmarks that we had inserted into every Rakgear backpack since I had started the company. On the bookmark was written the following scripture verse, with a picture of a bald eagle hovering over the words: "But they that wait on the Lord shall renew their strength; they shall mount up with wings as eagles, they shall run and not be weary, they shall walk and not faint." It was from the book of Isaiah in the Old Testament (NKJV). I made a vow when I first started Wickford Backpack Company, that every backpack shipped from our factory would include that bookmark. I carefully chose an Old Testament verse because it crossed over between Judaism and Christianity. It was my way of offering hope to every student that purchased a Rakgear Backpack. I wanted to inspire them, remind them, and reinforce the truth, that no matter what obstacles they would face in their young lives, there is a God Who is greater still. I sat down all alone that night after everyone had gone home and just stared at the bookmark. Then I realized that from the beginning, I was never in this business alone. I didn't come this far just because I was a shrewd businessman and a hard worker. I came this far because God had always had His hand in my life. Throughout my successes and failures, He was always there. Throughout my rebellious days, He was always there. He was with me. He gave me the best wife in the world. He blessed me with three beautiful children. He was there when Shayna was born. He was there when I was in the Hi Beams. He was there when I was a stock and bond broker. He was there when I built millions of dollars worth of homes, when everyone thought that I was a lunatic for starting North American Homes. He was there when I was selling thousands of dollars worth of fruit, produce, and flowers, at the open air stand on Park Avenue. He was there the night I stared out of the window at my brother's restaurant. He was there when I was bull raking with my brother, Al. He was always faithful, even when I wasn't. Why wouldn't He be there for me now? The answer was as clear as the nose on my face. HE WAS THERE!

The second thing that I did was call on a faithful friend that I had met at a trade show just one year earlier. His name was Young Suk. He was a fine Korean gentleman with a deep faith in God to match his bubbly personality. As soon as I told him of my dilemma, he quickly said, "We pray right now."

Then he said, "I have good idea, I know how you can fill Walgreens' order without coming up with $300,000. You may have to come up with $30,000, but not $300,000."

I immediately said, "How do I do that, Young, put up my house and my first born child?"

He responded, "You of little faith, listen to me. You buy two airline tickets to Korea for you and me. Don't delay! We leave next week. We go to my good friend's factory and mold maker. You bring Walgreens purchase order. They will make twenty- four thousand backpacks and twenty four thousand racks on your good word, on Walgreens' purchase order, and on lots of prayer."

I immediately ordered the tickets through our travel agent. I found myself on Korean Airlines heading for Seoul, South Korea seven days later, with Young Suk sitting next to me, smiling from ear to ear.

Seoul, South Korea was very different from China. Seoul is a metropolitan city, with a great skyline. Unfortunately, the air pollution there was comparable to China's. The yellow sand that blows in from Mongolia, causes the thousands of people walking the streets to wear those white dust masks. The Korean people were beautiful. But, the food did a number on my stomach. It was by far, the spiciest that I had ever eaten. The barb wire fencing, the army personnel and the 38th parallel separating North and South Korea, caused quite an eerie feeling in me.

Young Suk and I wasted no time in visiting the two factories, one that would be manufacturing the backpacks and one, manufacturing the injection mold. Together, they would produce the twenty-four thousand racks needed. I had a stainless steel injection mold already in China, but it was cost prohibitive to ship the racks to Korea and then pay to have them installed. For five days, Young introduced me to the most honorable businessmen that I had ever met. We thoroughly went over every type of material needed for the backpacks, including fabric, colors, zippers, zipper pulls, webbing, handles, shoulder straps and padding. In the end, they did exactly what Young said they would do. They only asked for $30,000 to make $300,000 worth of product. Naturally they wanted to see the Walgreens purchase order, but in the end, it came down to my word and a handshake. Now, the greatest obstacle to overcome would be meeting the June 19 deadline from Walgreens. I flew back home on Korean Air alone and Young stayed behind for another week to visit some family and oversee the project, making sure everything proceeded as scheduled.

I came home with a new glimmer of hope, but it was short-lived as Paul went over the upcoming bills, past due bills and expenses. We both scratched our heads. We realized even shipping all twenty-four thousand units on time to Walgreens wasn't going to get us in the black until we could collect ninety days later. With the financial pressures mounting and further exacerbated by the relentless pressure from my partners who just wanted out, my stress levels were reaching an all-time high.

All was not lost, however. We had shopped our business plan around and received some very strong interest in May 2002. It turned out that a gentleman from New York liked our plan. He specialized in debt financing and raising capital and felt he had very strong interest to raise three million dollars for us. It would be enough to buy our partners out and give us a good influx of working capital and certainly give us some breathing room. Coupled with the Walgreens order, it was enough to keep our hopes up. The biggest problem with the three-million-dollar debenture was the staggering monthly payments! Once again, I said to Paul, "It's do or die! We need to do it!" We agreed to move full speed ahead.

With the day-to-day pressures still mounting, Ana walked into my office. I had just hung up the phone, talking with Paul, and hearing some more not so great news regarding some long overdue bills. She said to me in her El Salvadoran accent, "Matt, Jerry is on the phone. He's the man who owns the rep group in Andover, Massachusetts. You already cancelled two appointments with him."

I said to her in a very distraught tone, "Ana please, the last thing we need right now is another rep group, just tell him that I can't meet with him or speak with him."

Within twenty seconds of Ana leaving my office, my direct line rang. It was Jerry. "Matt, how are you? It's Jerry, why don't you want to meet with me? You cancelled two appointments. I really like your product and I believe that I can help you."

I said very politely, "Jerry, to tell you the truth, I really don't need another rep group for New England and right now I'm swamped trying to meet a deadline for Walgreens."

Jerry was persistent and quickly said, "Matt, just meet with me! It can't hurt to just come up to my office in Andover. Let me show you our operation. How's next Wednesday at 10 A.M.?"

I just said to myself, "This guy just doesn't give up, or take no for an answer." I replied, "I'll be there."

In the back of my mind, I really planned on canceling for a third time. But when next Wednesday came around, I found myself driving to Andover, Massachusetts with a frown on my face. I thought to myself, "Why am I doing this? I've got so many more important things to do."

Two hours later, I arrived at Jerry's office building. I was surprised to find such a nice building. It was a decent size too, for a manufacturers' rep group in New England. I walked into the reception area and there was a professional free standing sign like one you would see in a hotel lobby. It said, "Welcome, Matt Olerio, from Rakgear."

The receptionist led me into a beautiful conference room with a very long, shiny mahogany table. She politely said, "Jerry and the rest of the group will be right in, make yourself comfortable."

I just thought to myself, "This guy isn't running any small-time rep firm here. This guy really has his act together."

Soon Jerry entered the room, a very well-dressed, very tall, distinguished gentleman in his late fifties. He gave me a big smile and a firm handshake and said enthusiastically, "I'm glad you didn't cancel this appointment. The entire group will be here shortly."

Within ten minutes, I found myself giving a full-blown Rakgear presentation to a crowded room of manufacturer reps that worked under Jerry. Three were his sons and several well-seasoned reps that covered other areas stretching all the way from Philadelphia to Florida.

The meeting and the energy from the group were far beyond anything I had expected. When I finished my presentation and was preparing to leave, the room cleared out and Jerry and I talked together. We had really hit it off. We made one of those instant friendships. There was just something about him that made you know he was a straight shooter and stand-up guy. I shook his hand ready to leave and he looked me right in the eyes and said, "I really like your product! Besides repping your line, are you looking for any investors?"

I almost spit my coffee out all over his suit, as I smiled and said, "Yes, as a matter of fact, I am. But to tell you the truth, cash flow is tight! I'm about to float a three-million-dollar debenture any day now."

Again, he looked me straight in my eyes, with his hand on my shoulder, and firmly said, "Don't do anything! I'm very close friends with the chairman of the board for Targus Group International. His name is Howard Johnson. This is right up his alley. He's currently on the hunt to break into the educational sector and acquire companies that could catapult them into that market. Rakgear is a perfect fit. Can you get me a business plan right away?"

I said with a big smile, "I can get you a business plan right now, I just happen to have one in my car."

Just as I was pulling away and saying my final good-byes, once again, Jerry reaffirmed his commitment to me and reminded me once more, "Remember, don't do anything until you hear from me."

The last thing I said to him as I started my car was, "Are they acquiring any other companies right now?"

He said, "Confidentially, between you and me, they're in the process of buying a company called Roundhouse. They make Glacier Gear lunch bags, cooler bags and CD Projects."

I looked at him, nodded and said, "I'm familiar with the company."

I drove away in absolute shock. Yet, as excited as I was, I had learned not to put the cart before the horse. So I called Paul, and said with very little emotion, "We might have a buyer for Rakgear."

All the way home I kept laughing to myself, "Glacier Gear lunch and cooler bags; what are the odds of that happening?"

In the back of my mind, I was thinking, "Well maybe Jerry was exaggerating a bit. Maybe he's just an acquaintance and not a close friend of the chairman of the board. After all, Targus is the largest manufacturer and distributor of computer carrying cases and portable accessories in the world, I mean, we're talking one powerhouse of a company." I just couldn't believe it.

Two days later, I was sitting at my desk and my secretary buzzed my line. "Matt, there's a Howard Johnson on line one who would like to speak with you. He said that you would know what it's in reference to."

I almost fell back in my chair and quickly shouted, "Put him through." I picked up the line, said, "Hello Howard, this is Matt." It all began.

"Matt, Howard Johnson, heard a lot of good things about you. Jerry speaks very highly of you. I love your product line! I spent hours looking over your business plan, I'd love to come into Rhode Island on Monday, bring some of my associates, have dinner and see your operation. I can tell you right now, I'm very interested."

I responded as cool, calm-and-collected as I could, "Howard, Monday will be great! I look forward to meeting you."

I hung up the phone and looked over at the bookmark that I had pinned to the wall in my office. "But they that wait upon the Lord shall renew their strength, they shall mount up with wings as eagles, they shall run and not be weary, they shall walk and not faint." Isaiah 40:30 (NKJV)

I then called Margie, my dad, and Paul, in that order.

Thirty days later, Targus Group International acquired Wickford Backpack Company for three million dollars in cash and stock, and offered me a three-year contract, allowing me to keep on Corey, Ana, and some other key employees. Today Rakgear is sold worldwide in over forty countries and continues to earn market share with new and spectacular cutting edge designs and features.

Rakgear, it was my dream that I watched come true, a dream that I could share with my wife, children, and family. But Rakgear is far from being the final chapter of my life and by no means designates that my life of dreaming and pursuing the desires of my heart are over. There is so much more that I want to accomplish and it goes far beyond money and glory. I'm thankful to have had the privilege to write this book. My greatest hopes are that you open your mind to all the endless possibilities for your own life, and then act on those possibilities with confidence and courage. And, if just one sentence or one word in this book ignited that spark in you, then I have accomplished what I set out to do from the very moment that I decided to write about a life filled with Mellow Peaches.

    I was lying awake in bed the other night at 3:00 AM just staring at the ceiling; Margie turned to me and said. ....?

Final Thoughts and Conclusion

What about your dreams? Is your truck still three-fourths full, or have I given you enough "fruit for thought" to get up the courage to follow your heart's desire? Your greatest dreams will unfold before your eyes the very moment that you take those first few steps, the very moment you realize that being afraid is OK, and that "going for it" involves risk, sacrifice, and perseverance. But what a great reward awaits those of you who learn to take your greatest fears and transform them into faith, hope, and action. That's when you start to move mountains, find your purpose, and realize that the real meaning of success goes far beyond making money and acquiring "things." I believe there is no stopping you from accomplishing your greatest dreams, not because of any rousing, motivational words that I have written in this book, but rather on account of what you have found out about yourself as you read through these chapters. If you want it, then go after it, and never stop believing in it. I know you'll find exactly what you've been searching for and so much more. I will leave you with a quote from a man named Joe Olerio, my father, who taught me a valuable life lesson at an early age, and inspired me to be all that I can be. He said, "DON'T EVER COME HOME WITH A FULL TRUCK AGAIN!"

It seems a simple, yet powerful, and profound statement to make. Yet, too many dream seekers never summon the courage to roll down the window and shout, "Mellow Peaches, Three Pounds for a Dollar," and let it all out, to see their dream through. They never stick to the plan or acquire the determination, perseverance, courage, and consistency needed to sell out the entire load, and empty the truck. When you finally decide that you will never again come home with your truck still three-fourths full, it will be at that time when you roll down the window of your heart, and shout out from roof tops, "I CAN DO IT!"

My dad's words stay with me always, as a constant reminder, and mean far more to me than just being successful in business, far more to me that just making money. I have applied those words to every aspect of what I felt was the true meaning of success for my life: success as a husband, as a father, as a son, as a brother, as a neighbor, as a friend and as a man who's not afraid to speak of the awesome wonders of God. Empty your mind if it's filled with doubt and fear. These thoughts overcome you and deceive you out of all you were meant to be and accomplish in this life. When you can put aside your fears and press forward, that's when it all begins and your life takes on a whole new meaning of excitement and adventure. Seek and dream the greatest dreams and watch them all come true, right before your eyes.

Remember, there are three types of people in this world…which one are you?

I wish you great success in everything you attempt in your life. May God richly bless you in all ways, and fulfill the desires of your heart.

I CAN DO IT, I WILL DO IT, IT IS DONE!

You Can't Win If You Don't Run !

Maybe you didn't have a dad like mine who instilled and fostered your entrepreneurial spirit. That doesn't mean it's too late to acquire that spirit within you. There is a heavenly Father Who sees all the potential and giftings that He placed in you from the moment that He called you into existence. The exact same traits of perseverance and industriousness and believing in yourself that I have in me, are in you. Don't focus another day or another minute on what you didn't have, or opportunities that weren't available, or the lack of a positive role model in your life. Instead, let's take all those ingredients and put them to work for you. Let's start laying down railroad tracks, covering some serious ground, everyday. All those obstacles and emotions from your past will no longer stop you from moving forward because you're going to put them to work for you, rather than letting them be the impediments that they've been in your life. It's time to find out just what Godly talents have been lying dormant in you. Awaken them!!!

I want you to lay out a rough plan that's directly related to your goals. Use my example as a guideline and then write out your own detailed, thirty day plan. These are the small steps that lead you to the larger steps, that lead you to the starting line, where the race to succeed begins. **You can't win if you don't run!**

Example:

The Dream: To see my [fictitious] tulip bulb invention which can plant up to twelve bulbs at a time in one quick easy motion become a reality and sell millions of units to American gardeners.

My Rough Plan:

Pray often.
Secure the initial financing to get my project off the ground.
Get some referrals for some reputable patent attorneys.
Call the patent attorneys' offices and get the ball rolling.

Get a confidentiality agreement signed from them and submit about how much money is needed for a patent search to see if anyone else in the world has my idea.

Give my product a name, perhaps "Tulip Tapper." Submit it to the trademark attorney who works in the same office as my patent attorney. Ask for a name search on my proposed product name.

Develop a logo, meet with a graphic design company that's creative and can assist me in developing a cool logo and slick tag line. Perhaps, "Tulip Tapper" "One tap, One push, and watch 'em grow"

Find a marketing/design company [start with the Yellow Pages] to start developing some packaging for retail that is eye catching, tells the story, and creates an emotional response for the consumer and helps drive "the brand." Tulip Tapper, the one and only, the original.

Make some connections with some overseas factories and at home to have prototypes made up of the "Tulip Tapper." (Visit local college/university import/export departments for assistance and manufactures names that would best fit my project.)

<u>Discuss my idea with as few people as possible.</u>

Sit down with my accountant and develop a sound business plan to raise venture capital money or submit my business plan to my bank and apply for a small business loan.(SBA)

Acquire press for my nifty invention, have a PR strategy. Go to local newspapers and TV stations.

I will pursue having my product aired on QVC Network and Home Shopping Network.

Research manufacturing representative companies. Do I need a manufacturer's rep group or should I go it alone for now? Where can I find some reputable manufacture's rep groups to cover certain geographical areas of the country? On the Internet? Chamber of Commerce? From retail chain buyers?

Go on the Internet and learn about importing goods from overseas. How do I obtain a customs broker? Where is the closest shipping port to my business or home?

Can I rent some cheap warehouse space until I get rolling, or should I just work out of my basement and garage until my cash flow allows otherwise?

Do I need to incorporate? Call an accountant and an attorney. Open up a business checking account.

Call the phone company and have a separate line installed so I can keep my business calls separate from my home line and not disturb my family.

What does "patent pending" mean, and how long does it take to actually receive a full fledged patent? What is the difference between a design patent and a utility patent?

Within thirty days be completely set up with an office (desk, supplies, phone lines, computer, UPS pick ups, etc.).

Apply for a UPC bar code number.

Designate time for my family.

Pray often.

My Goal: To complete all of the above within the next thirty days.

Your Rough Plan

_____
_____
_____

Next, list key people, agencies, and business associates with whom you are going to surround yourself. Start looking at all the needs associated with your dream. Break them down into categories. Assign a specific person[s] who you believe can be instrumental in moving things along in the right direction. I'm not a Hillary Clinton fan. But, in the case of pursuing your dreams and reaching your goals, it does "take an entire village." Formulate your own village of key people.

Now you need to act on your dreams and goals. Remember, up until now, we've been taking small shovels of dirt to dig the ten foot hole. Let's start thinking about hiring a backhoe. From this point on, we're moving into overdrive. You need to make seven key appointments this week. They may include your accountant, a personal trainer, a real estate broker, a banker, a venture capital group, your pastor, a patent attorney, an architect, a web site designer, a business man who owns a building or land that you're interested in, a college/university for enrollment, or/and you immediate family. Do not procrastinate another day.

List your seven key appointments:

FOOTPRINTS

One night a man had a dream. He dreamed he was walking along the beach with the LORD.

Across the sky flashed scenes of his life. He noticed two sets of footprints in the sand.

When the last scene of his life flashed before him he noticed that many times there were only one set of footprints.

He also noticed that it was at the very lowest times in his life.

He questioned the LORD about it. "LORD, You said that once I decided to follow You You'd walk with me all the way. But I have noticed there is only one set of footprints. I don't understand why, when I needed You most You would leave me."

The LORD replied, "My precious child, I love you and would never leave you. During your times of trial and suffering, when you see only one set of footprints, it was then that I carried you."

Author, Unknown

Printed in the United States
16410LVS00002B/97-1011